Becoming a Woman of Wild Joy:

Discover the Surprising Delights
of Marriage, Motherhood, and Life Mission

366-Day Inspirational Journal
Five-Year Memory Book

By:
Mrs. Valerie Christina Malicki, MA, LPCC, CPM

Copyright 2023. All rights reserved. No part of this book may be reproduced in any form without written permission of the copyright owners. Every effort has been made to ensure that credits accurately comply with information extensively researched. We apologize for any inaccuracies that may have unintentionally occurred. We will resolve inaccurate or missing information (kindly brought to our attention) in a subsequent reprinting of this book. If you find a mistake, please contact the publisher at malickisix@gmail.com. Thank you!

The author does give permission for social media posts of others using this book! Please give full credit with this reference note: #womanofwildjoy. Many thanks!

ISBN 979-8-9857631-0-2 E-book
ISBN 979-8-9857631-1-9 Paperback
ISBN 979-8-9857631-2-6 Hardback

Scripture referenced as NIV taken from New International Version. Scripture quotations taken from *The Holy Bible*, New International Version, NIV. Copyright 1973, 1978, 1984, 2011 by Biblica, Inc. Used by permission. All rights reserved worldwide.

Scripture referenced as NLT are taken from the *Holy Bible*, New Living Translation, copyright 1996, 2004, 2015 by Tyndale House Foundation. Used by permission of Tyndale House Publishers, Inc., Carol Stream, Illinois 60188. All rights reserved.

Scripture referenced as TMT (The Message Translation) taken from *THE MESSAGE*, copyright 1993, 1994, 1996, 200, 2011, 2002. Used by permission of NavPress Publishing Group. Represented by Tyndale House Publishers, Inc., Carol Stream, Illinois 60188.

Scripture referenced as TPT are from The Passion Translation. Copyright 2017, 2018 by Passion &Fire Ministries, Inc. Used by permission. All rights reserved. ThePassionTranslation.com

This book is dedicated to my family:
The Malicki Six. The Malicki Six includes:
my husband, Russ, myself, and our biggest blessings
—our four children:
Rosie, Violet, Milo, and Lilac Malicki.

This book is dedicated to our future grandchildren. I can't wait to create new memories and remember all the laughing, living, and loving that we have shared together. I can't wait to have all our family gathered around the table, enjoying Dad's gourmet cooking! Hopefully, we will have to tell our grandchildren the same admonition that we did our children: no reading books or singing silly songs at the table. Haha. And hopefully you grandchildren will do lots of both…as long as you wait till we are finished with our scrumptious dinner conversation and meal!
I love you all, our grandchildren, already!

This book is dedicated to the girls and boys of the next generation. May The God of The Universe give you audacious boldness to live with Wild Joy as a King or Queen in His Heavenly Kingdom!

This book is dedicated to every reader who chooses Wild Joy on her journey. May you be daughters of The King who are blessed,
and who are a blessing!

The Story In Me

"If a story is in you, it has to come out."
—William Faulkner

Over five years ago, I began my own secret journey seeking transformation and Joy (although, I didn't really know it at the time). Joy is capitalized here because even in my darker days, I knew I needed Divine Joy. This is something much more profound than social media likes, a good hair day, money, sex (even great sex), power (even good power, as in the power to "do good"), status (even very popular symbols of status), or whatever "goody" was offered to me from "out there." I, somehow, intuitively, knew that I needed an inner transformation. Somehow, I knew this was what I needed, and that it would ripple out into my whole outward life. My own transformation would ripple out into my love life, and into my legacy. Some people call this intuitive knowing. But I will say that somehow I deeply knew this.

My life had become rather messy—on the inside. On the outside, things looked quite good. I was married to a good man (though I wasn't so sure, in all my sleep deprivation), and we had three healthy children, each of whom I wanted immensely (and each of whom were driving me nuts).

Despite how good things looked, I felt like I lived in a padded prison—confined, and worse, empty, empty, empty. Why? This was the question I was forced to ask myself. If I was "living my dream," why did I feel so…blah?

I was forced to begin evaluating my life and exploring my own story. I say "forced" because I knew my life had to change—

when you identify immediately with the word "famine," this is a problem. My life was undergoing a personal famine, but I knew I wanted to live in overflow, abundance, and yes, Joy. At the time, it seemed like an average person saying they wanted to climb Mount Everest. I had a long way to go, and a lot to learn—especially about my own story.

Over the last five years, I chose to be a cherished wife and homesteading, homeschooling mother of four in the Midwest. I was hidden, meaning I began living, loving, and laughing more than engaging with the madness of the outside world and "being visible" in the online world. I tuned out the madness of the outside world in so many ways. I chose to unplug often, and focus on actual positive change from the inside out. I also tuned out the naysayers, my own fears, and all the voices raining on my "Wild Joy" parade.

For me, experiencing Wild Joy is a Divine experience. Wild Joy is from God and will therefore be capitalized to reflect its Divine nature. Anything that is from God is capitalized in this book, as this points to the Divine nature of God.

As I sought out true Joy, I began to realize this Truth over and over: God is my Joy. God became my secret Joy. Knowing God gives me Wild Joy. No one and nothing can take this Wild Joy away. God gives me more Joy than anything I have ever, ever, ever experienced, from money to sex, from power to relationships, from higher education to marriage. God gives me even more Joy than motherhood, and these days, motherhood brings me many sweet moments.

Wild Joy feels truly exhilarating, and there are no ill side effects. This Joy includes going to bed with a clear conscience, knowing I am in good standing with God and with others. I experience Joy in knowing I have done what I can, and that is enough.

This Wild Joy saw me through the horrible grief of losing my younger sister. I feel true Joy knowing that her cancer-ridden body is restored in heaven. Yes, even death cannot conquer this Joy, because, once again, this Joy is from God. We will explore this and many facets of Joy together, day by day, month by month.

I began to experience that Wild Joy *is* true Joy. Joy from God became the only thing that wildly transformed my entire life. Each day is a Wild Joy adventure in itself. Each day is a new day to continue with this wild transformation. I know it because I live it in the depths of my being. And I know it because Wild Joy is the only true Joy that sustains me through all life's ups, downs, arounds, joys, sorrows, rages, calms, and even pleasant surprises. (Surprises, even pleasant ones, can require some adjustments!)

This is all part of why I am writing this book. This book is for you, and for me, to keep finding our answers. This journal is for us to actually experience Wild Joy. Yes, it is an adventure of the soul, and it is a process. Some reflections may be vague, a feeling, a nudge. Sometimes the answers will be specific, like, "You need to set a boundary here, or this will ultimately drive you mad." Sometimes the answers will be a mix of both, like, "It's OK to let the kids watch another video. You desperately need this time with your hubs, and it is available now." You will get the idea of increasing your self-awareness as we journey on together.

I will note in the prompts some of the reflections and guided questions that led me to experience Joy—yes, Wild Joy.

Especially in the beginning of my own Joy adventure, it seemed there were so many factors that were able to quench my Joy experience—from stress to conflicts to the constant sleep deprivation newborns bring. It was essential for me to focus on experiencing Joy every day. One day at a time, they say. So, one day at a time is what we will do together.

This journal is written to support you, my brave friend, in experiencing this Wild Joy. This journal has daily inspiration (365 days, plus February 29), for five years. These daily Joy prompts summarize the essential practices that have brought me Joy.

Thanks to these essential practices, I am experiencing true intimacy in my satisfying and committed marriage, even through the ups and downs. I am homeschooling and enjoying our four children immensely. I am actually living a life of Wild Joy, in too many ways to describe, right now. Thank God, my life has experienced a wild transformation. Wild Joy elevates my life, love, and legacy every day.

Does this all sound a little crazy, a little far-fetched? Good! This Wild Joy adventure destination is living a daily life that is beyond your wildest imagination…you will see!

The great joys and great trials of my life have deepened me, and have expanded my life. I feel in my heart that these Joy practices need to be shared, and I want to share them with you. Perhaps you will then be able to avoid some of the greatest trials I have experienced. That is my prayer. I also pray that you will be inspired to reach even higher heights than I have, in love, success, health, or whatever areas you desire.

This book is a culmination of my two decades of personal work as an educator, coach, and therapist with people of various cultures from around the globe.

When I was 17, I began taking classes at Wheaton College in human development, spirituality, and soul care. This was the beginning of my first soul adventure, though I didn't know it at the time. Later on, after graduate school, I began my work as a Licensed Professional Clinical Counselor. This was about two decades ago.

Yet, for all my extensive training in education, coaching, and counseling, I still wanted answers. Despite my professional certifications, I still wanted Joy answers. I wanted, and desperately needed, some insight into my experience of yearning for Joy.

In my own Joy adventure, I discovered that having God with me, and journeying in life with Him, gives me all the Joy I need. Life is not all sunshine and rainbows—true. Yet, knowing God is with me changes everything. God and I are co-creators of each day of Wild Joy.

I am a mentor, and mentors always want the absolute best for their mentees. So, this is why I share my heart. As you begin, keep in mind that sometimes the guideposts we will discuss will feel raw, vulnerable, challenging, or perhaps even funny. A full life is expressive of all this. Yes, ALL THAT is part of this magnificent Wild Joy experience.

Let's learn together to experience this true Joy, little by little, over the course of this journey.

Yes, this Joy experience grows little by little by little, and it is a process that occurs over the course of many moons. So, come along, friend. I am excited for all that is in store on our Wild Joy discovery journey!

"So perhaps the best thing to do is to stop writing Introductions and get on with the book."
—A.A. Milne

The Story In You

This journal is the true story of my own great trials, and my own great joys. It is also the story of *your* own great trials, and *your* own great joys. This book is a strong hand with just-right warmth that is gently holding yours as we adventure together.

This journal is a unique guide, as it is *also* a guide that you write for yourself. Your personal journal contains your own life experiences of ordinary and extraordinary, of pain and passion, of trial and triumph.

It is designed for you to create, dream, explore, and document your heart's desires. It is also a sacred place of self-care, a place where you can document your personal adventures of replenishing, rejuvenating, and strengthening your body, mind, heart, and soul. My friend, this journal is for you to envision and experience Wild Joy in daily life as you willingly commit to this process, day by day.

Experiencing Wild Joy *is a process*. There are times we overestimate the empowerment, transformation, and Wild Joy that can be experienced within a shorter period of time, yet drastically underestimate the revolutionary change that can occur over a five-year period.

This is why this journal is a guided five-year adventure. You will be amazed at how much your life can transform in 60 short months.

Especially after being a mother for over a decade now, it is almost mind-blowing how everything can wildly *change*:

children, mental health, attitudes, babies, empowerment (or lack thereof), bodies, physical health, people, work, finances, experiences, vacations, spiritual health, marriage, myself, free time (or lack thereof)—yes, everything! Change over a five-year period is often slow, yet can be quite dramatic, in an amazing way, if we are intentional.

The purpose of this journal is to intentionally allow for reflection, transformation, and yes, intentionally experiencing Wild Joy.

It's almost impossible to explain, but as you commit to this process, you will experience more empowerment, transformation, and Wild Joy day by day. You will see, day by day, as we journey together

Finally, as we begin our journey together, I invite us both to commit to the process.

My commitment: to be your Wild Joy mentor.

Your commitment: to use this guided journal as many days and weeks as possible as you bravely open yourself up to experiencing more and more Wild Joy on your own unique soul adventure.

I invite you to commit to taking at least a few moments on most (if not, all) days, and—with a special focus on each month's exercise—to use your journal daily. Let this journal be your daily tool to help you focus on the exhilaration of experiencing Wild Joy.

Personal Note To Reader

Dear Friend,

One sentence a day for five years. Where will your path twist and turn over the next five years? What will you experience on your own soul adventure? Imagine what new, wild, and wonderful experiences we may create along our Wild Joy adventure together. I am so excited for all the Wild Joy you will experience. Without further ado, let's begin experiencing Wild Joy, ASAP (as in, right now)! One day at a time…here we go!

With Wild Joy, Your Friend,

Valerie

CEO and Founder,
Eve's Joy Professional Mentoring
EvesJoy.com

**DISCLAIMER: Eve's Joy Professional Mentoring exists for educational, inspirational, and mentoring purposes <u>only</u>. This book is written for education, inspiration, and mentoring purposes <u>only</u>. No part of this book, or any of Eve's Joy mentoring services, are intended to diagnose or treat mental or emotional disorders. Thank you for using this book and Eve's Joy Professional Mentoring as intended, exclusively for mentoring, education, and inspiration.

**DISCLAIMER regarding all references: I am a passionate lover of Truth in all forms. All Truth is God's Truth. God speaks to me through all things and people in His world. No reference implies an endorsement of the beliefs, practices, preferences, religion, or opinions of the person, group, culture, religion, or connections to the noted reference. The references are for reflection and inspiration <u>only</u>. Please remember that God could use a donkey to speak to Balaam. It is also essential to remember that all Truth IS God's Truth, and to search for Truth, with an open heart, within the pages of this book. God promises that if we seek, we will find. To be clear, this collection of inspiration is intended to inspire women, not to endorse various groups, circumstances, opinions, or people. Thank you in advance for experiencing this book as intended, exclusively for mentoring, education, and inspiration.

How To Use This Journal:

1. Each month has a brief reflection focus exercise. This is followed by a focus statement, or mantra, for the month. A mantra is simply a statement to remember each day. This statement affirms your daily and monthly focus. I invite you to simply ponder this mantra all month long, as it uniquely fits your life. The monthly mantra will be one part of guiding you toward experiencing Wild Joy.

2. Each day, write yourself a one-sentence reflection. (You may also draw, color, or doodle if that fits better for you, according to each day. Every day has a line and a bit of space for you to reflect, dream, process, and expreeeess! Whee!) You can begin your journal in any month, on any day. Simply open to the month you wish to start in, and complete the one-sentence exercise that begins each month. Next, let this exercise be your focus for the remainder of that month. This means, with the monthly focus exercise in mind, you will write a one-sentence reflection every day for the remainder of the month. When the month is over, simply move on to the next month. Since this journal is all about learning to embrace your pace, starting on the day and month that works for your unique life is perfect. For example, if you receive this as a birthday gift on December 19, simply complete the monthly focus exercise for December, then complete the rest of December, one day at a time. Then, move on to January. Every month will weave together seamlessly and guide you into greater Wild Joy, wherever you begin.

3. Write the sentence that easily comes to you. You can journal about the topic of the month and the daily thought prompt—or not. Let your journaling and your sentences flow effortlessly, according to what you are experiencing. Your sentence can express a feeling, a special event, a frustration, a gratitude memory—really, anything you want to remember. Writing just one sentence a day makes this unique journal very doable. I see all the plates you are spinning; I am spinning them, too. Let your journal work for your own unique life, needs, style, and wishes. This is *your* journal. That means if you get off track, it is A-OK. Really. This is your own soul adventure. Embrace your pace. This reflection is about what is easily coming to your awareness. Each day, simply track the personal insights you are gaining. I am standing for you, as you are one step closer, each day, to transforming your life with Wild Joy.

4. Examples of one-sentence reflections:
    - "Today, I woke up so angry because I went to bed super late...note to self...don't do that again. Not worth it!"
    - "Wow, I always thought fairy tales were for other people, so it's really a stretch for me to imagine my own life this way."
    - "I am pinching myself that I am a mom of four and a happy wife—dreams do come true!"
    - "Today was my anniversary, wow, have the years flown by...here's to many more!"
    - "This month's theme is daring. I can't remember the last time I felt daring."
    - "I love the quote of today—I will be repeating it to myself as a mantra to further celebrate my Joy!"

5. When you complete the first year, simply continue on to the next year, following the dates. Use your journal for the second year, and so on, writing below your previous entries. Each date contains a place for five sentences—one sentence for each year. You can reflect back on the past year with each entry. (It's wonderful to see how far you've come!)

6. After five years, your personal journal will hold five years of your own special memories, reflections, soul adventures, difficult learning experiences, notes to self, and lots of Wild Joy experiences. In this way, your journal creates your own unique, five-year record.

7. This journal and Joy adventure is for *you*. Enjoy the process and allow yourself to experience more and more Wild Joy every day. Over time, your set point for experiencing good things, satisfying soul adventures, and especially Wild Joy will only increase. I invite you to welcome this positive change and relish every moment, success, and Wild Joy experience. I invite you to welcome mind-blowing transformation, and yes, Wild Joy!

Thank you for journeying together! I am super excited for all the future holds as we experience the exhilaration of Wild Joy—together.

Table of Contents

JANUARY: Desiring 19

FEBRUARY: Clarifying 55

MARCH: Mentoring 89

APRIL: Connecting 127

MAY: Attaching 163

JUNE: Working 197

JULY: Repairing 233

AUGUST: Daring 269

SEPTEMBER: Rising 305

OCTOBER: Soaring 339

NOVEMBER: Nesting 373

DECEMBER: Celebrating 407

JANUARY

Become a Woman of Wild Joy Through *Desiring*.

"Desire is a
mighty force, one of your
most divine attributes! Whatsoever
things ye desire when ye pray, believe that ye have
received them and ye shall have them! See the Godlike
quality of desire. For it is part of the Atomic energy of the
soul. The Kingdom of Heaven within you is operated through
desire. Do not quench it or crush it or suppress it. Rather offer
it to Me. Offer Me your most elementary desires, your craving
for happiness, for love, for self-expression, for well-being, for
success, for joy, on any level of your being—offer these freely
and without shame to Me and I will transmute them
so that you shall achieve release and fulfillment
and complete freedom from frustration."
—John Gaynor Banks,
The Master and Disciple[1]

---

1. John Gaynor Banks, The Master and Disciple (St. Paul, MN: Macalester Park Publishing, 1954).

What desire within you yearns to experience fulfillment? Do you yearn for free time? Quiet? Sweet, romantic intimacy? Simple friendship? Time spent unplugged, in nature? A sense of belonging? Appreciation and acceptance? Less stress? Increased loving intimacy? Emotional connection? Financial success and freedom? Physical health? Peace?

Whatever you are desiring most these days, I invite you to acknowledge it, here. I invite you to focus on *one* desire this month. What is your desire? Simply finish this sentence, below, today and every consecutive year, as you see fit.

My heart's desire is:

20__ _____

20__ _____

20__ _____

20__ _____

20__ _____

Mrs. Valerie Christina Malicki, MA, LPCC, CPM

Whatever you are desiring is OK.
Truly! As you give your desire to God, He refines your desire and, like a good father, gives good gifts. A desire may be anything, from practical —such as a new vehicle—to spiritual—such as moving on from the past by growing in forgiveness. For me, in the past I have desired: more money, less stress, more free time, less fighting, more intimacy, less constant nurturing of others' needs, more long country walks, hiking near waterfalls, et cetera, et cetera, et cetera!
Nothing is off limits. Really!

Each day,
ponder the prompt
of the day and answer with a
simple one-sentence reflection. Your one
-sentence reflection may sound like this: "Wow,
I never thought God cared much about my bank account—
is that really spiritual?" or, "I am so inspired to pray about
my real life and desires, maybe God will answer my
prayers after all," or, "I want a baby!" or, "I am on
the fence about having babies—right now,
my focus is on living (and loving) my
total life mission."

This journal is for you, so share
whatever authentic reflection comes to your heart.

Let's make this focus on *desire* simple. Each day for the rest of January, write a one-sentence reflection on your desire. Let the daily prompt allow you to expand your vision of all that is possible. Allow your one-sentence reflection to flow easily with whatever comes to you. This is *your* journal, a safe place to express your thoughts, your feelings, and—most especially—your reflections on your desire.

Anticipation about receiving one desire can be the sweetest motivation!

This month, each day, let's remember a mantra:

**I become a woman of Wild Joy
through *desiring*.**

Mrs. Valerie Christina Malicki, MA, LPCC, CPM

January 1

Today, let's expand your named desire.
Take time to BE for 15 minutes. BE still, and imagine your desire fully. As you imagine your desire today, how does it look, smell, sound,
taste, and feel?

20__ _____

20__ _____

20__ _____

20__ _____

20__ _____

January 2

Let's expand your named desire even more. For example, when I desired more financial prosperity for our family, I also wanted financial prosperity that was aligned with our skills, values, and priorities. There are plenty of ways to gain money, but I actually wanted more than just money. I wanted to be present with our four young children. I wanted to see my husband nightly. I hoped for meaningful work for my family within our skill sets. Within this framework, our family businesses and our family itself have continually experienced more and more financial prosperity. This is just one example of expanding a desire.

Let's expand *your* named desire. What are three aspects of your desire that could expand your named desire even more? Let's add to your vision of desire by writing your answers below. We will continue to expand your desire all month. Right now, simply finish the next sentence. My heart's desire also includes:

20__ _____

20__ _____

20__ _____

20__ _____

20__ _____

Mrs. Valerie Christina Malicki, MA, LPCC, CPM

January 3
Visualizing is a
powerful form of planning!
Next, let's visualize an experience of you fully receiving your desire. I am giving you full permission to dream, imagine, create, and celebrate successes all along your journey. You certainly don't need my permission, but I do know the feeling of wanting
to receive permission.

As you envision receiving your newly expanded desire, what do you hear, smell, taste, feel, and see? Write a one-sentence reflection about your experience, here:

20__ _____

20__ _____

20__ _____

20__ _____

20__ _____

January 4

It has been said that only dead people want nothing. I understand this to mean that if I am alive—*really* alive—I have desires, and that is more than OK. In fact, it is wonderful! Let's reframe desire as something *wonderful.* When you consider your desire, give *yourself* permission to have it.

Today, let's reflect—and fully imagine—this wonderful experience with a receptive focus and mantra: I allow myself to receive my heart's desire!

20__ _____

20__ _____

20__ _____

20__ _____

20__ _____

Mrs. Valerie Christina Malicki, MA, LPCC, CPM

January 5
"Take delight in the Lord, and
he will give you the desires of your heart."
—Psalms 37:4, NIV

20__ _____

20__ _____

20__ _____

20__ _____

20__ _____

January 6

One way to take delight in God is trust Him with our heartfelt desires. I trust that every desire brings me back to God, because He gave me the ability to even *have* a desire. He created all pleasures—sensual, spiritual, and everything in between. I have found that, as I give my desire fully to God and then refocus back on delighting in God (especially through simple gratitude), He gives me the desires of my heart. As only a good Father could give, He gives good gifts. He has graciously given me my family, my faithful husband, our four children, our beloved country-living home life, and so much more. These are just some of the unique gifts from His Loving Hand.

What are you thankful for, today?

20__ _____

20__ _____

20__ _____

20__ _____

20__ _____

Mrs. Valerie Christina Malicki, MA, LPCC, CPM

January 7

"Every good and perfect gift is from above,
coming down from the Father of the heavenly lights,
who does not change like
shifting shadows."
—James 1:17, NIV

20__ _____

20__ _____

20__ _____

20__ _____

20__ _____

January 8

We can access the power of Almighty God through prayer. Prayer is, simply, calling out to God. With His Omnipotent Power, He can do anything when we call out to Him in prayer. That's even better than a magic wand!

God multiplies all we bring to Him. One example is when I gave Him my vulnerable desire to feel deeply loved. He gave that desire back to me, and so much more. Yesterday, I had my four little kids cuddling me and spontaneously giving me butterfly kisses. We were all giggling so hard! God has shown me that He can truly do anything. He took my simple desire to be loved and gave me a fun, big, and loving family.

20__ _____

20__ _____

20__ _____

20__ _____

20__ _____

Mrs. Valerie Christina Malicki, MA, LPCC, CPM

January 9
"Ah, Sovereign Lord, you have made the heavens and the earth by your great power and outstretched arm. Nothing is too hard for you."
—Jeremiah 32:17, NIV

20__ _____

20__ _____

20__ _____

20__ _____

20__ _____

January 10

"To exist is to change,
to change is to mature, to mature is to go on creating oneself endlessly."
—Henri Bergson

20__ _____

20__ _____

20__ _____

20__ _____

20__ _____

Mrs. Valerie Christina Malicki, MA, LPCC, CPM

January 11

Over the years, my experiences of changing and maturing have also changed my desire to be loved. It is interesting to see how God has purified my own desires over the years. At the same time, He has given me more than I ever imagined. Change can be such a good thing!

What have been your own experiences of changing and maturing, especially in regards to your desire?

20__ _____

20__ _____

20__ _____

20__ _____

20__ _____

January 12

When flying on a plane, we are taught that, before we should help anyone else, we must first put on our *own* oxygen mask. In the same way, healthy self-care helps you BREATHE *first*. Once you are able to breathe, yourself, then—and only then—can you help others. I love to give myself "self-care oxygen" by having some alone time in prayer, or enjoying a long country walk, or relaxing and laughing with fun, celebration times. A healthy self-care practice simply entails any experience where you take good care of yourself, emotionally, spiritually, physically, or mentally. Self-care helps me refuel. With self-care practices in place daily, I can allow myself to experience good physical, emotional, spiritual, and mental health. Then, I DO have something of value to offer those around me.

20__ _____

20__ _____

20__ _____

20__ _____

20__ _____

Mrs. Valerie Christina Malicki, MA, LPCC, CPM

January 13
"Honor, cherish and nourish yourself."
—Brandon Bays

As a wife and mom, this is essential to remember. I am daily surrounded by the needs of others, as well as my own very real needs: physical, emotional, spiritual, and mental health needs. I know I can't *give* what I don't *have*. Healthy self-care practices give me oxygen to keep on keeping on with: nurturing, caring, supporting, and truly loving. It has been said:
"You gotta nourish to flourish."

20__ _____

20__ _____

20__ _____

20__ _____

20__ _____

January 14

These days, I enjoy lots of healthy self-care practices: prayer time, sunshine, fun drinks and snacks with my kids, reading and snuggling with my kids, kisses and hugs and snuggles with my hubs, a long country walk, an easy nutritious dinner, and a flexible, relaxing family schedule. Healthy self-care practices every day keep me going strong!

How do you need to put on your own oxygen mask, first, with self-care? I invite you to experience at least one healthy self-care practice today.

20__ _____

20__ _____

20__ _____

20__ _____

20__ _____

Mrs. Valerie Christina Malicki, MA, LPCC, CPM

January 15

Eventually, self-care became an essential aspect of my daily routine. At the most painful point of my journey, I was in what could have been called a "soul famine." A soul famine is when one feels very depleted and burned-out, emotionally, mentally, spiritually, and physically. It took a season of intense self-care to fill back up—a lot of water to make the dry ground flourish again. As a result of this growth experience, daily self-care is now a part of my own daily "work." Showing up in life with a healthy mind, body, and soul is the best way that I can truly love.

What is one *daily* healthy self-care practice that would nourish your mind, body, or soul?

20__ _____

20__ _____

20__ _____

20__ _____

20__ _____

January 16

"Practice your work every day.
Then, let no thought, no man, no woman, no mate, no friend, no religion, no job, and no crabbed voice force you into famine."
—Clarissa Pinkola Estes, Ph.D.,
Women Who Run With Wolves[2]

20__ _____

20__ _____

20__ _____

20__ _____

20__ _____

---

2. Clarissa Pinkola Estés, Ph.D., ***Women Who Run With Wolves*** (New York: Ballantine Books, 1992).

Mrs. Valerie Christina Malicki, MA, LPCC, CPM

January 17
"It is never too late for a new beginning in your life."
—Joyce Meyer

20__ _____

20__ _____

20__ _____

20__ _____

20__ _____

January 18

As I gave my desires to God, He fulfilled my every desire—in His way, and in His time. Remembering God's past faithfulness to me gives me courage to keep giving my desires to Him. As I gave God my own yearnings—from a saintly desire for spiritual impact to a more human desire for some free time—I have experienced God giving my desires back in return, a hundredfold. He has helped me to build a therapy career, to become a wife and then become a mom, to focus on homeschooling our four children, and to create our family's businesses. He has never let me down. Having the courage to offer my desires to God has all been worth it.

20__ _____

20__ _____

20__ _____

20__ _____

20__ _____

January 19
"What on earth would become
of me if I should ever grow brave?"
—Patti Callahan,
Becoming Mrs. Lewis[3]

20__ _____

20__ _____

20__ _____

20__ _____

20__ _____

---

3. Patti Callahan Henry, ***Becoming Mrs. Lewis*** (Nashville, TN: Thomas Nelson, registered trademark of HarperCollins Christian Publishing, Inc., 2018).

January 20

As I bravely made changes in my life, I began to spend more time focused on my positive passions, such as voracious reading, being near water, and scheduling in some rest and relaxation time. I balanced my passions with needs—like laundry and dishes—as well as fun moments, like picking summer peaches with my family. When I rejuvenate well, I feel like I am having a love affair with life. The positive changes just feel good, in my body, mind, and soul.

What is one way you may focus on your positive passions and rejuvenate your body, mind, and/or soul, today?

20__ _____

20__ _____

20__ _____

20__ _____

20__ _____

January 21

"No one has ever said that life is easy, but it is easier if you love it. If you hate your life it becomes impossible to live."
—Eddie Jaku,
The Happiest Man on Earth:
The Beautiful Life of an Auschwitz Survivor[4]

20__ _____

20__ _____

20__ _____

20__ _____

20__ _____

---

4. Eddie Jaku, ***The Happiest Man On Earth: The Beautiful Life of an Auschwitz Survivor***, (New York, NY: Harper an Imprint of HarperCollins Publishers, 2021).

January 22
"Start by doing what is necessary, then what is possible, and suddenly you are doing the impossible."
—St. Francis Of Assisi

20__ _____

20__ _____

20__ _____

20__ _____

20__ _____

Mrs. Valerie Christina Malicki, MA, LPCC, CPM

January 23

When I wanted my fourth baby, I imagined having hot cocoa and enjoying cozy family snuggles after a fun, snowball-filled day with our four kids. As I gave my desire for a big family to God, He definitely gave me back my desire—and so much more. For me, a big family is a big adventure, every day. It's wild, yet wonderful, and I'm thankful for the special, "butterfly kisses" moments. Family life is not all "rainbows and sunshine," yet I am thankful for the everyday, routine moments of regular, everyday life, too. Meals together, memories made with beloved pets, reading classic books, and having silly moments with goofy sibling antics are all a part of this magnificent package. Yes, my heart's desire has definitely been granted—*a hundredfold.*

Imagine *your* unique desire being given back to you a hundredfold. What do you imagine you would hear, smell, taste, feel, and see?

20__ _____

20__ _____

20__ _____

20__ _____

20__ _____

January 24

"Sometimes I am asked to speak to young people...They want to know how I discovered the will of God...I tell these earnest kids that the will of God is always *different* from what they expect, always *bigger*, and, ultimately, infinitely more *glorious* than their wildest imaginings."
—Elisabeth Elliot[5]

20__ _____

20__ _____

20__ _____

20__ _____

20__ _____

---

5. Elisabeth Elliot, ***Keep a Quiet Heart*** (Ann Arbor, Michigan: Vine Books, Servant Publications, 1995).

Mrs. Valerie Christina Malicki, MA, LPCC, CPM

January 25

What is one way you have already experienced aspects of your desire in the past—maybe even in this month? For me, as I sought financial prosperity, I recalled times in my past when money came to me. I felt the feeling of abundance and savored this feeling. I imagined experiencing this abundant feeling again. All this prepared me to receive my desire. My desire did find me! There were trials that led to the triumphs, yes, but prosperity did come. I began enjoying my desire for financial prosperity, as well as all my desires, from a place of abundance and trust.

I invite you to imagine enjoying your desire today from a place of abundance and trust. How does this feel?!

20__ _____

20__ _____

20__ _____

20__ _____

20__ _____

January 26
"It's delightful when your imaginations come true,
isn't it?"
—L.M. Montgomery,
A Novel Journal: Anne of Green Gables[6]

20__ _____

20__ _____

20__ _____

20__ _____

20__ _____

---

6. Montgomery, Lucy Maude, ***A Novel Journal: Anne of Green Gables***, (San Diego, CA: Canterbury Classics, An imprint of Printers Row Publishing Group, 2016).

January 27

"The starting point of all achievement is DESIRE…Weak desire brings weak results, just as a small fire makes a small amount of heat."
—Napoleon Hill

20__ _____

20__ _____

20__ _____

20__ _____

20__ _____

January 28

"Champions aren't made in the gyms.
Champions are made from something they have deep inside them—a desire, a dream, a vision."
—Muhammad Ali

In what way will your desire
require you to be a champion?

20__ _____

20__ _____

20__ _____

20__ _____

20__ _____

January 29

Imagine the fulfillment of your desire multiplied by 100. This is often uncomfortable, but imagine fully receiving your desire, expanded exponentially. I invite you to stretch your comfort zone and imagine receiving the bliss of your desire, expanded 100 times. Visualize and feel this experience fully. What are you hearing, smelling, tasting, feeling, and seeing, now?

20__ _____

20__ _____

20__ _____

20__ _____

20__ _____

January 30
Reflect today on one closing
thought about the powerful nature of your desire:

My desire is the divine, atomic energy of the soul!

20__ _____

20__ _____

20__ _____

20__ _____

20__ _____

Mrs. Valerie Christina Malicki, MA, LPCC, CPM

January 31

Notice how your desires are experienced, fulfilled, received, and ever-changing, as the days—and even years—go by. This reflection experience can be incredibly empowering. When I read old journals about wanting to be a wife and mom, about other life goals, and about lots of other desires, too, it is sometimes hard to believe: *desires really do come true!*

As the month of intense focus on desire is coming to a close, let's pause and reflect, together. What is the most essential lesson you have learned, or are learning, about your own unique desire? I invite you to write it below.

20__ _____

20__ _____

20__ _____

20__ _____

20__ _____

At Eve's Joy Professional Mentoring,
we specialize in pastoral care for women only.

We offer a unique, world-class blend of
faith-based, therapeutically-informed, certified professional
mentoring.

We would love to hear more about your unique *desiring vision*, and also provide you with specific next steps on how to continue to make it happen.

Simply drop us your current one-sentence *desiring vision* at EvesJoy.com. You can leave your confidential vision at the bottom of the home page where it says "Leave a message." With this simple entry, you apply to receive one of our periodic, free, confidential, exploration calls. An exploration call is guaranteed to be the best next step toward creating your own unique *desiring vision*.

Your completely confidential response helps
us to create content that further supports you, such as:
blogs, emails, webinars, summit/retreat topics, new online
groups, podcasts, et cetera.

We are constantly creating new supportive
content for you. Please drop us a line, and let us know how
we can support your next step toward becoming
a woman of Wild Joy!

FEBRUARY

Become a Woman of Wild Joy Through *Clarifying*.

"'Would you tell me, please, which way I ought to go from here?'

'That depends a good deal on where you want to get to,' said the Cat.

'I don't much care where,' said Alice.

'Then it doesn't matter which way you go,' said the Cat.

'...So long as I get somewhere,' Alice added as an explanation.

'Oh, you're sure to do that,' said the Cat, 'if you only walk long enough.'"

—Lewis Carroll, ***Alice in Wonderland***[7]

Think about your own life story, for a moment. What "way" do you want it to go?

---

7. https://www.goodreads.com/quotes/449586-alice-would-you-tell-me-please-which-way-i-ought Accessed 13 August 2022.

Take 15 minutes to just BE. BE still.
BE quiet. BE, and imagine your ideal life. BE, and imagine living your ideal life in five years. Imagine exactly all that you hope for in your work, play, and love. Imagine experiencing the Wild Joy of inner happiness and healthy, harmonious balance. Imagine wild successes, time freedom, mind freedom, money freedom. Imagine living out your wildest, personal, and unique callings and gifts. Take these moments to tune out the naysayers and the "shoulda, coulda, woulda" regrets, and move forward.
Let's focus, this month, on experiencing
Wild Joy through *clarifying*.

The point of this entire month is to bring expanded clarity into your life. You may yearn for more free time, more children, to be married, to have a more fulfilling career, less stress, or...anything. This month helps you to become *clear* on what you need and want most in the smorgasbord of life. This clarity, then, provides a map for "where you want to go." In sum, *clarity* gives you wisdom to *know* where you *do* want to go!

Mrs. Valerie Christina Malicki, MA, LPCC, CPM

Simply complete the following
sentence, today, and then each consecutive year.

As I clarify what I most want my life to
be like in five years, right now, it is this:

20__ _____

20__ _____

20__ _____

20__ _____

20__ _____

This is your *clear vision* for today. This is
our focus this month. Each day this month, simply write
a one-sentence reflection as we expand your *clear vision*
together.

This month, let's remember our
mantra each day:

**I become a woman of Wild Joy
through *clarifying*.**

February 1

At one point in my own journey, I
realized I desperately needed clarity. I was
at a crossroads with many milestone decisions regarding
my career, my children, my marriage, and even my faith.
Was God with me? What was God speaking to me? How
could I be clear-minded and clear-hearted in a noisy,
busy world? What would this even be like?
I needed wisdom.

This month we focus on
your *clear vision*. In what area of life do you
most need clarity, today?

20__ _____

20__ _____

20__ _____

20__ _____

20__ _____

Mrs. Valerie Christina Malicki, MA, LPCC, CPM

February 2

"Light, space, zest—that's God! So,
with him on my side I'm fearless, afraid of no
one, and nothing. That's the only quiet, secure
place in a noisy world. The perfect getaway, far
from the buzz of traffic."
—Psalm 27, TMT

20___ _____

20___ _____

20___ _____

20___ _____

20___ _____

February 3

What if experiencing God really is a zesty, perfect getaway? I know my prayer times are definitely quiet, secure, strengthening places in a noisy world. I gain immense clarity from God when I spend time in prayer. I love when I can unplug, spend time away from needs and others, grab my favorite (caffeinated) beverage, my Bible, and my journal. For me, this is how I experience God as a zesty, perfect getaway!

20__ _____

20__ _____

20__ _____

20__ _____

20__ _____

February 4

Spending time in prayer and in God's Presence brings me great clarity. I love to listen for God's voice and to write down how God is speaking to me. In this way, my journal becomes a record of how God is working, moving, and answering my prayers. This sounds like a supernatural experience—because it is. It is difficult to describe, but very real to my heart. God speaks to me, especially through the Bible—and in a gentle whisper, which I know is His Voice.

20__ _____

20__ _____

20__ _____

20__ _____

20__ _____

February 5

"Cry for help and you'll find it's grace and more grace. The moment he hears, he'll answer. Just as the Master kept you alive during the hard times, he'll keep your teacher alive and present among you. Your teacher will be right there, local and on the job, urging you on whenever you wander left or right: 'This is the right road. Walk down this road.'"
—Isaiah 30:19-22, TMT

20__ _____

20__ _____

20__ _____

20__ _____

20__ _____

February 6

"When we need help we wish we knew somebody who is wise enough to tell us what to do, reachable when we need him, and even able to help us. God is Omniscient, Omnipresent, Omnipotent —everything we need."
—Elisabeth Elliot,
Keep a Quiet Heart[8]

20__ _____

20__ _____

20__ _____

20__ _____

20__ _____

---

8. Elisabeth Elliot, ***Keep a Quiet Heart*** (Ann Arbor, Michigan: Vine Books, Servant Publications, 1995).

February 7

"Omniscient" is just a fancy word for "all-knowing." What would it be like to know someone who is "all-knowing"? Does this sound supernatural? (Yes, it is. And, having a supernaturally Wise friend is truly Divine!)

What have been your past experiences of reaching out to God? In what area do you want God to reveal His All-Knowing Clarity into your life today?

20__ _____

20__ _____

20__ _____

20__ _____

20__ _____

Mrs. Valerie Christina Malicki, MA, LPCC, CPM

February 8

Clarity is all about wisdom, discernment, and guidance. I definitely need all of this in regards to my milestone decisions in life, such as in my marriage. As I gain clarity, more and more, I realize that yes, I do want to keep on keeping on with creating a happy marriage with my husband. Yes, yes, yes, even through the "imperfectly perfect" times of conflict resolution. As we resolve conflicts well, ultimately our marriage strengthens. I am thankful for God's wisdom, discernment, and guidance to help me navigate marriage issues, and all my decisions in life.

20__ _____

20__ _____

20__ _____

20__ _____

20__ _____

February 9

For me, milestone decisions are ones that significantly alter the course of life. For me, I definitely considered motherhood—or not—for a while. When I was young, it seemed I was too busy with my career and life in general. Was it to be, or not to be? I put it off for several years, until it really hit me: yes, by golly, I definitely wanted to be a mother. I would say marriage, divorce, children, and big moves of location or vocation are all milestone decisions. Milestone decisions permanently alter the course of life in meaningful ways.

20__ _____

20__ _____

20__ _____

20__ _____

20__ _____

Mrs. Valerie Christina Malicki, MA, LPCC, CPM

February 10

When my hubs quit his job after 15 years as a faithful employee to start his own company, it was a milestone decision. Navigating decisions with our family businesses are the milestone decisions our family is facing these days. These business decisions revolve around our entire family's desire to homeschool. This is a milestone decision that we continue to navigate, as we know it will have a large and long-term impact on all our lives.

What milestone decisions are you facing, and/or focused on, today?

20__ _____

20__ _____

20__ _____

20__ _____

20__ _____

February 11

Finding spaces, places, and times to
meet with God in still, quiet prayer allows me to find clarity.
I definitely need this practice firmly in place when making
milestone decisions. I need quiet, space, prayer,
and time spent listening to God.

How will you find space, quiet, and time to
meet with God today?

20__ _____

20__ _____

20__ _____

20__ _____

20__ _____

Mrs. Valerie Christina Malicki, MA, LPCC, CPM

February 12
"Be still and know that I am God."
—Psalm 46:10, NIV

I love to seek guidance on little things—or, seemingly little things. Every fall, it seems, I suddenly realize, oh my, our son has no clothes! (He often grows so quickly from one year to the next, and in the Midwest, children need different clothes for each season.) Since I am often late in ordering, a lot of times I end up buying clothes on clearance. Whew. Win! God even works this out. Having clothes for my kids is actually something God helps me to juggle when I have space and time to really listen. I find this listening prayer to be essential to thriving in my daily life. I juggle a lot, and yearn to thrive through it all. As I am still, and seek God for clarity, it all falls into place!

20__ _____

20__ _____

20__ _____

20__ _____

20__ _____

February 13

"And as Elijah stood there, the Lord passed by, and a mighty windstorm hit the mountain. It was such a terrible blast that the rocks were torn loose, but the Lord was not in the wind. After the wind there was an earthquake, but the Lord was not in the earthquake. And after the earthquake there was a fire, but the Lord was not in the fire. And after the fire there was the sound of a gentle whisper."
—I Kings 19:11b-12, NLT

20__ _____

20__ _____

20__ _____

20__ _____

20__ _____

February 14

I began a practice of listening to the sound of God's gentle whisper by totally unplugging in the quiet. If at all possible, I like being near dirt, ground, grass, trees, sand, water, or sky when I pray. For me, it draws me closer to God—just as Elijah heard God speak to him in a gentle whisper when he was by himself in the wilderness. Often, even just a window with a view of the sun, sky, and trees helps me to listen and connect with my Creator. On my own journey, the more I listened with intention to The Voice of God, the more clarity and wisdom I gained. This wisdom helps me to know deeply that, yes, God was and is with me—ALWAYS. I know deeply that He never leaves me; it is I who wander, at times, from His Loving Presence.

20__ _____

20__ _____

20__ _____

20__ _____

20__ _____

February 15

"No great work has ever been produced except after a long interval of still and musing meditation."
—William Bagehot

20__ _____

20__ _____

20__ _____

20__ _____

20__ _____

Mrs. Valerie Christina Malicki, MA, LPCC, CPM

February 16

I have experienced seasons in my life that contained many long intervals of still and musing meditation—especially when I was pregnant and birthing babies. Nine months of sweet, still pregnancy produced a whole new, great work—a new little family member to have and hold—our baby! This first "incubation period" brought me into an entirely new season: the season of motherhood. These days, I'm enjoying my dream and am grateful for our four babies!

20__ _____

20__ _____

20__ _____

20__ _____

20__ _____

February 17

In your own life, in what ways have you ever experienced a long interval of still and musing meditation that later produced a great work? This may be a successful business project, a home purchase, a new business endeavor, writing a book, developing a loving relationship, a successful move of location, completing your high school, vocational, or college education, or perhaps the fulfillment of a memorable vacation or "bucket list" experience.

How have you had a long interval of preparation that produced a "great work"?

20__ _____

20__ _____

20__ _____

20__ _____

20__ _____

Mrs. Valerie Christina Malicki, MA, LPCC, CPM

February 18

"Pregnant and birthing mothers are elemental forces, in the same sense that gravity, thunderstorms, earthquakes, and hurricanes are elemental forces. In order to understand the laws of their energy flow, you have to love and respect them for their magnificence at the same time that you study them with the accuracy of a true scientist."
—Ina May Gaskin,
Spiritual Midwifery[9]

20__ _____

20__ _____

20__ _____

20__ _____

20__ _____

---

[9] https://www.azquotes.com/quote/858086 Accessed 29 May 2022.

February 19

Although I have experienced actual
pregnancies, I have also experienced
other, nontraditional pregnancies. I still do,
all the time. For example, I am pregnant with
a vision for our home life. I am pregnant with
ideas. I am pregnant with projects. I continue to be
pregnant with dreams. All these different kinds of
pregnancies follow the same pattern: they incubate
for a time, then, *voila!* They are born. In this way,
I will always experience pregnant seasons. New
ideas, and new adventures will always be in
my heart. One by one, new creative ideas
will incubate and, then, be born
—all in good time!

20__ _____

20__ _____

20__ _____

20__ _____

20__ _____

Mrs. Valerie Christina Malicki, MA, LPCC, CPM

February 20

These days, how would you like to be "pregnant" with a new idea, project, adventure, or "baby"? What clarity do you need about having a successful birth with this new "baby"?

20__ _____

20__ _____

20__ _____

20__ _____

20__ _____

February 21

There are seasons in which my visions are incubating *well* beneath the surface. Just because nothing is seen "above ground" doesn't mean that nothing is happening "below ground." My own *clear vision* was, and is today, a process of growth. Projects, ideas, dreams, and plans may require invisible growth for a season before there is a visible "baby bump."

20__ _____

20__ _____

20__ _____

20__ _____

20__ _____

Mrs. Valerie Christina Malicki, MA, LPCC, CPM

February 22

I experienced a process of "incubating" growth when we were working toward building lucrative family businesses. Thankfully, these days we are enjoying the "baby" of thriving businesses.

In what stage of development is your baby, whether it is an actual baby or a new "dream baby"?

20__ _____

20__ _____

20__ _____

20__ _____

20__ _____

February 23

My eldest daughter is ten. I am amazed at the miracle of her own life and how she continues to bloom, blossom, and grow. When I see her offer to read storybooks to all her siblings, my heart swells with Wild Joy. The seeds my hubby and I have planted are growing into a beautiful forest. At times, the process has felt slow. Yet, the long-term rewards are all worth it. Clarity and confidence in my mothering grows, more and more, as I nurture and create loving family times each day.

20__ _____

20__ _____

20__ _____

20__ _____

20__ _____

February 24

"If you hear a voice within you say 'you cannot paint,' then by all means, paint, and that voice will be silenced."
—Vincent Van Gogh

20__ _____

20__ _____

20__ _____

20__ _____

20__ _____

February 25

When I consider gaining clarity, I remember:
if only I am present to listen, God's Voice will clearly guide me with All-Knowing wisdom! What is one thing—big or small—that you need clarity about? (I do find, with God, there is no "big" or "small.") It could be anything, from where to buy needed clothing or when to finish a work project. It could be discovering ways to engage in a difficult situation, or how to best handle
a stressful task.

How do you *specifically* need All-Knowing wisdom today?

20__ _____

20__ _____

20__ _____

20__ _____

20__ _____

Mrs. Valerie Christina Malicki, MA, LPCC, CPM

February 26

This month, we have focused on experiencing Wild Joy through clarifying. What is your own clear vision, now? Ponder how you yearn to experience your life in five years. Ponder the way you yearn to feel, and all you hear, smell, taste, and see in your daily life. Then, answer this next question.

As I clarify what I most want my life to be like in the next five years, right now, it is this:

20__ _____

20__ _____

20__ _____

20__ _____

20__ _____

February 27

"In the journal I do not just express myself more openly than I could to any person; I create myself."
—Susan Sontag

20__ _____

20__ _____

20__ _____

20__ _____

20__ _____

Mrs. Valerie Christina Malicki, MA, LPCC, CPM

February 28

"You'll get a brand new name straight from the mouth of God. You'll be a stunning crown in the palm of God's hand...And as a bridegroom is happy in his bride, so your God is happy with you."
—Isaiah 62, TMT

20__ _____

20__ _____

20__ _____

20__ _____

20__ _____

February 29

Today is a rare day in life—one that only happens once every four years, of course. On this special day, I invite you to ask God: "How am I rare and special to you, God?" If you are feeling especially brave, I invite you to ask Him to give you *a new name,* as described yesterday in Isaiah 62. God has answered this prayer of mine on special occasions, though (being God and all), He can answer prayer whenever and however He chooses. Yet, if we tune our ears to listen, He is actually *always* speaking a healing, affirming, loving word. He has called me "Cherished," "Friend," and "Blessed," in some of our most special times. It is *amazing* to consider being a friend with The God of The Universe!

I invite you to ask God to speak to you in an extra special way, today. What healing, affirming, loving word is God speaking to you, today?

20__ _____

20__ _____

Mrs. Valerie Christina Malicki, MA, LPCC, CPM

At Eve's Joy Professional Mentoring
we specialize in pastoral care for women only.

We offer a unique, world-class blend of faith-based,
therapeutically-informed, certified
professional mentoring.

We would love to hear more about your unique *clear vision*,
and also provide you with specific *next steps* on how to
continue to make it happen.

Simply drop us your current one-sentence
clear vision at EvesJoy.com. You can leave your
confidential vision at the bottom of the home page where it
says "Leave a message." With this simple entry, you apply
to receive one of our periodic, free, confidential, exploration
calls. An exploration call is guaranteed to be the best next
step toward creating your own
unique *clear vision*.

Your completely confidential response helps
us to create content that further supports you, such as:
blogs, emails, webinars, summit/retreat topics, new online
groups, podcasts, et cetera.

We are constantly creating new supportive
content for you. Please drop us a line and let us know how
we can support your next step toward becoming a woman
of Wild Joy!

MARCH

**Become a Woman of Wild Joy
through *Mentoring*.**

"As Naya Nuki ran, she was so busy paying attention to her efforts, that she forgot her fears."

"Naya Nuki knew that she was looking at the shining mountains of her homeland. She danced around a big rock with great joy and excitement. She was going to make it after all! Nothing would stop her now! Naya Nuki was the happiest girl in the world. She danced and danced with joy."

"Naya Nuki's story would be repeated by many Indians around campfires for years to come as this girl and her journey to freedom would
become a legend."

"So it was that Sacajawea and Naya Nuki, met again on this happy and historic day."

—Kenneth Thomasma,
selected portions from a book in
his Amazing Indian Children series,
titled ***Naya Nuki: Shoshoni Girl Who Ran***[10]

---

10. Kenneth Thomasma, ***Naya Nuki: Shoshoni Girl Who Ran*** (Jackson, WY: Grandview Publishing Company, 1983).

Naya Nuki's amazing true story is shared in oral tribal history, as well as the travel logs of the Lewis and Clark Expedition. Naya Nuki was kidnapped and made into a slave by an enemy tribe at age 11. She escaped solo and traveled 1000 miles by foot to her freedom. Again, though it is hard to believe, this amazing true story is documented in history and told in oral tribal history. Lucky for us, because we can learn from her incredible journey to freedom!

Mentors, like Naya Nuki, are "exemplars." They are role models who demonstrate courage and virtue, and inspire others to do the same.

This amazing little girl walked and ran 1000 miles alone. She literally freed herself from forced slavery. She escaped, miraculously, to the freedom and loving kindness she experienced in her true tribe. Wow!

Mrs. Valerie Christina Malicki, MA, LPCC, CPM

This month, we focus on mentoring. We will remember various mentors of all ages and life experiences whose very lives inspire us.

Mentoring is exponentially powerful because it requires growing and learning from those who have *actually done* what we aim to do. Mentors do not talk about theories they know not of. They have *actually experienced* what we yearn for. This may be marital satisfaction, a positive family legacy, a healthy homeschool education, or *any* endeavor or experience. This may be creating elevated Joy in work or play. This may be creating a Joy-Filled family legacy. This may be leading a revolution in areas of education, justice, or reform of all types.

A good mentor is someone who you would be proud to be like one day. Mentors are exceptional and unique in all these ways.

Becoming a Woman of Wild Joy

Let's take 15 minutes to visualize, ponder, and imagine your answers to the statements below.

Then, simply write your answers below, this year, and then each consecutive year:

I choose to be a mentor who is:

20__ _____

20__ _____

20__ _____

20__ _____

20__ _____

Mrs. Valerie Christina Malicki, MA, LPCC, CPM

I am seeking a mentor who is:

20__ _____

20__ _____

20__ _____

20__ _____

20__ _____

This is our mentoring vision, and our focus for this month. As we focus on mentoring, we will also explore inspirational thoughts from leaders throughout history. Each day, simply note, in a one-sentence reflection, how this thought may apply to your own mentoring vision.

This month, remember our mantra each day:

I become a woman of Wild Joy through *mentoring*.

March 1

A mentor is an exemplar who inspires you to feel, "If they can do it, I can too." That is just one thing I love about Naya Nuki's 1000-mile journey. She was 11 years old, and she escaped by herself. Her solo 1000-mile walk took her along the rivers she knew well. Her audacious courage inspires me to have audacious courage. What an amazing girl!

In what way has someone inspired you to feel, "If they can do it, I can too?" How so?

20__ _____

20__ _____

20__ _____

20__ _____

20__ _____

Mrs. Valerie Christina Malicki, MA, LPCC, CPM

March 2

We each have different "1000-mile journeys to freedom" in life. I certainly felt this way when my marriage was in crisis. Working with mentors—those with thriving, joyful, connected marriages—made it possible for me to, eventually, experience a thriving, joyful connection in my own marriage. The restoration of my marriage was a unique "1000-mile journey" that was made possible through healthy mentorship.

20__ _____

20__ _____

20__ _____

20__ _____

20__ _____

March 3

Yes, when my marriage was struggling,
it was a game changer for me to connect
with women who had thriving marriages. Learning
from those who had more peace, connection, and passion
in their marriage exemplified for me how to have those
qualities in my own marriage. In this mentoring situation, I
learned lifelong and life-changing behaviors and habits. My
positive, more experienced mentors
changed my marriage, forever,
for the better.

20__ _____

20__ _____

20__ _____

20__ _____

20__ _____

Mrs. Valerie Christina Malicki, MA, LPCC, CPM

March 4

In a time of marital strife, having marriage mentors was deeply transformative. I learned from those who had what I wanted. This is a most *essential* quality in a mentor! Remembering this principle also helps you *steer clear of the advice and input, no matter how well-meaning, of those who do not have what you want.*

How have you been given terrible advice before? What happened? What did you learn?

20__ _____

20__ _____

20__ _____

20__ _____

20__ _____

March 5

Ironically, there are times when another person's entire life is like bad advice. Ouch, but that happens at times, for sure. Although it is tempting to dismiss people who are quite different, what might you learn? How might they be a counterintuitive mentor, showing you how *not* to be?

How have you experienced a counterintuitive mentor who was, at that time, a good "bad example?"

20__ _____

20__ _____

20__ _____

20__ _____

20__ _____

Mrs. Valerie Christina Malicki, MA, LPCC, CPM

March 6

A truly *good* mentor is much more than someone you admire, or even get along with well. They are a role model, also known as an exemplar, because *you would gladly trade lives with them*. An amazing mentor has the amazing life that you want. True mentorship is transformative, as you learn from those who have "climbed your mountain." This month, we can learn from the great joys and trials of those who have gone before us. We observe others, from the past and present, so that we may apply life lessons from their invaluable experiences.

Thus, an ideal mentor is actually miles ahead of you, *especially in the area in which you yearn to experience growth.*

20__ _____

20__ _____

20__ _____

20__ _____

20__ _____

March 7

As you consider your own unique life circumstances, what would be your own "1000-mile journey"? Would this be a journey of deep self-care, trauma recovery, or financial abundance? A spiritual journey of soul-searching, improving physical well-being, overcoming depression or anxiety, or experiencing true love? Or is it a new creative project, a new relationship, or cementing the kind of legacy you want to pass on?

How would you describe the "1000-mile journey" that is before *you*, these days?

20__ _____

20__ _____

20__ _____

20__ _____

20__ _____

Mrs. Valerie Christina Malicki, MA, LPCC, CPM

March 8

A good mentor for your own 1000-mile journey inspires specific qualities, such as courage or healthy relationships, by their own example. Also, a mentor could be one who inspires excellence in a specific skill, such as writing, business, mothering, or leadership, *through their example.* A mentor is simply a teacher, of any age, circumstance, role, or character quality, who is an *exemplar*—an example.

I invite you to ponder your own unique mentor vision. What is one specific quality that would be important for you to look for in a mentor these days? What do they have that you also want? (Reminder: it has been said that only dead people want nothing!)

20__ _____

20__ _____

20__ _____

20__ _____

20__ _____

March 9

"God is my Hope, my Joy, my Love, my Everything!"
—Violet Valentina Malicki

My eight-year-old daughter, Violet, inspires me daily in the specific area of faith. Her childlike heart has some of the strongest faith I have ever seen! I joke with those close with me that she has a special "in" with God. Although this is just a joke, she does seem to receive answers to her prayers in remarkable ways. This summer, she has an opportunity to go to summer camp. The doors seemed closed, and she kept praying. Then, the door was wide open. Trust me, I take notes on her bold faith!

20__ _____

20__ _____

20__ _____

20__ _____

20__ _____

Mrs. Valerie Christina Malicki, MA, LPCC, CPM

March 10

An excellent mentor may be, at first, an unlikely mentor. We homeschool our children, yet the learning definitely goes both ways. All my kids *teach me,* as they are strong faith and prayer warriors. They each have a powerful, childlike faith in their own unique way. Our kids do not have a PhD in theology, but they love God with all their hearts. I have to admit, the strength of their prayers and their genuine faith over fear is humbly inspiring!

Have you ever had a time where you experienced a mentor who was seemingly an unlikely leader?

20__ _____

20__ _____

20__ _____

20__ _____

20__ _____

March 11

Another way a mentor may, at first, *seem* unlikely is through their exemplary personal experiences, rather than their ideology, trainings, credentials, or status. For example, a person who has experienced financial prosperity, not a person who *teaches* financial prosperity. Another example may be a person who *experiences* a positive level of happy, healthy family functioning in their own life. This person would be a better mentor than someone with poor family experiences, even though they may have significant family therapy credentials from a high-status university.

What is one way a successful, experienced mentor is different from an inexperienced person (of any background, credentials, or status) who is offering advice or guidance? What are a few more specifics about the type of person who has already experienced your own "1000-mile journey" with *wild success*?

20__ _____

20__ _____

20__ _____

20__ _____

20__ _____

Mrs. Valerie Christina Malicki, MA, LPCC, CPM

March 12

In order to experience true mentorship with an inspiring, positive, challenging mentor, you may need to go on a special little journey to find that person. I know I have found amazing mentors, in real life, in the areas of work, career, mothering, marriage, mission, finances, etc., but only *after* I did my own due diligence of exerting time, money, and energy.

Often, one powerful mentor is the very best investment in experiencing my own personal success, and is better than any program or plan or impersonal form of help. A mentor can "hold your hand," so to speak. In my own life, the personal help of various mentors continues to be a priceless part of living my fullest destiny.

20__ _____

20__ _____

20__ _____

20__ _____

20__ _____

March 13

Now that you know what type of mentor you would love to have, what are you willing to invest—regarding time, money, and energy—to begin a powerful mentorship learning experience? Remember: your own growth and development is a wonderful investment, because it is an investment into *you,* of course. Your personal growth and development are *worthy* of investing in. There are times a vehicle needs new tires before there is a crash. We all need "regular maintenance" in various ways to keep moving forward. Having the support of a mentor can sometimes be like necessary, regular maintenance for *you.* What is one area that you would love support, in order to move forward in life?

20__ _____

20__ _____

20__ _____

20__ _____

20__ _____

Mrs. Valerie Christina Malicki, MA, LPCC, CPM

March 14
"It always seems impossible until it's done."
—Nelson Mandela

20__ _____

20__ _____

20__ _____

20__ _____

20__ _____

March 15

I like to discover mentors who have achieved "the impossible." This encompasses a wide range of experiences, from high achievement to overcoming tremendous obstacles. This also refers to joyfully transforming the ordinary into the extraordinary, especially with homeschooling. I have a dream of homeschooling my children and preparing them to be godly, positive, and flourishing adults. There are other home educators who have accomplished just this, and it inspires me. When I can, I love to learn from these brave souls!

What type of brave soul inspires you?

20__ _____

20__ _____

20__ _____

20__ _____

20__ _____

Mrs. Valerie Christina Malicki, MA, LPCC, CPM

March 16

The actual experiences of inspiring brave souls can be priceless. For example, one home educator shared how others were overly concerned for her children at times. She would be questioned, "What are the kids really learning? What about gaps?" Now that they are grown, two of her four kids are successful doctors, and the other two children have thriving career skills, and all have thriving families and lives. All her children are fulfilling their life's purpose. Looking back, she has zero regrets about the many sacrifices of home education. And her children all share that they appreciated having large chunks of quality family time and work and play—*all* at home sweet home. Yes, the knowledge and input from a mentor's real-life experience can be *invaluable*!

20__ _____

20__ _____

20__ _____

20__ _____

20__ _____

March 17
"A single dream is more
powerful than a thousand realities."
—J.R.R.Tolkien

20__ _____

20__ _____

20__ _____

20__ _____

20__ _____

Mrs. Valerie Christina Malicki, MA, LPCC, CPM

March 18

Have you ever considered that your own
life would be an *example* to others? What kind of example
do you wish to be, or not to be,
and why?

20__ _____

20__ _____

20__ _____

20__ _____

20__ _____

March 19
"One child, one teacher,
one book, one pen can change the world."
—Malala Yousafzai

(What if that person is *you*? How might
your life uniquely and positively impact
the world, every day?)

20__ _____

20__ _____

20__ _____

20__ _____

20__ _____

March 20

"The woman who follows the crowd
will usually go no further than the crowd.
The woman who walks alone is likely to find herself in
places no one has been before."
—Albert Einstein[11]

20__ _____

20__ _____

20__ _____

20__ _____

20__ _____

---

11. https://wisdomquotes.com/loneliness-quotes/ Accessed 11 December 2021.

March 21

"The thing that makes
you exceptional, if you are at all,
is inevitably that which makes you lonely."
—Lorraine Hansberry

Have you ever considered loneliness—or a
feeling of "being in Wilderness," so to speak, and alone—
as being a sign of being exceptional?
Why or why not?

20__ _____

20__ _____

20__ _____

20__ _____

20__ _____

March 22

"Men, it has been well said, think in herds;
it will be seen that they go mad in herds, while they only
recover their senses slowly, one by one."
—Charles Mackay

Have you ever felt the joy of "missing out"
from "activities of the herd"? Have you ever experienced an
awakening that seemed to set you apart?
Why or why not?

20__ _____

20__ _____

20__ _____

20__ _____

20__ _____

March 23

What may it be like to "recover your senses" from herd-type thinking? How may this feel, and look, in your own unique life? How would you describe your own life, currently—part of the mad herd, or as recovering from cultural forms of senselessness? In what areas of life, or in what ways, would you love for a mentor to help you "recover your senses," and awaken to more Wild Joy?

20__ _____

20__ _____

20__ _____

20__ _____

20__ _____

Mrs. Valerie Christina Malicki, MA, LPCC, CPM

March 24

I love learning from all the mentors in my life—past and present—about what brings them joy. For example, my grandmother was a very positive, kind, outgoing, and joyful matriarch. I can hear Grandmother Smith sharing that, "Your children are the joy of your life."

Who—or what—is an example, or experience, that teaches you about experiencing joy in life?

20__ _____

20__ _____

20__ _____

20__ _____

20__ _____

March 25

"If I have seen further than others,
it is by standing upon the shoulders of giants."
—Isaac Newton

For one thing, this idea is talking about learning from the experiences of others. The best learning happens when one can learn from a true exemplar.

What is one more way you hope to learn from a true exemplar?

20__ _____

20__ _____

20__ _____

20__ _____

20__ _____

March 26

We are all here today because we are standing on the shoulders of those who have gone before us. As we observe the lives of those around us, and those lives recorded in history, we learn. For example, I personally have an interest in World War II because I believe it contains powerful lessons for us, personally and collectively.

What is one way that "giant mentors," past and present, *inspire* you?

20__ _____

20__ _____

20__ _____

20__ _____

20__ _____

March 27

"Somebody, after all, had to make a start.
What we wrote and said is also believed by many others.
They just don't dare express
themselves as we did."
—Sophie Scholl

Sophie Scholl was a young German woman
killed by guillotine, by the Nazis, for standing for freedom
for all Germans with her secretly distributed pamphlets
advocating for *Freiheit* (German for "freedom"). Today,
there are memorials in Germany which remember
and honor her immensely inspirational
courage in a dark time in history.[12]

20__ _____

20__ _____

20__ _____

20__ _____

20__ _____

---

12. https://www.lewrockwell.com/1970/01/jacob-hornberger/the-white-rose/ Accessed 11 December 2021.

Mrs. Valerie Christina Malicki, MA, LPCC, CPM

March 28
"The only thing necessary for the triumph of evil is for good men to do nothing."
—Edmund Burke

20__ _____

20__ _____

20__ _____

20__ _____

20__ _____

March 29

"It is the sisters and wives and mothers,
you know, Caddie, who keep the world sweet and
beautiful...It's a big task, too, Caddie—harder than cutting
trees or building mills or damming rivers.
It takes nerve and courage and patience,
but good women have those things."
—Carol Ryrie Brink,
Caddie Woodlawn[13]

20__ _____

20__ _____

20__ _____

20__ _____

20__ _____

---

13. Carol Ryrie Brink, ***Caddie Woodlawn*** (New York, NY: Aladdin Paperbacks, An imprint of Simon & Schuster Children's Publishing Division, First Aladdin Paperbacks Edition, 1990).

March 30

"Your life stands tall as a tower, like a shining light on a hill. Your revelation eyes are pure, like pools of refreshing—sparkling light for a multitude. Such discernment surrounds you, protecting you from the enemy's advance. Redeeming love crowns you as royalty. Your thoughts are full of life, wisdom, and virtue. Even a king is held captive by your beauty."
—Song of Songs 7:4-5, TPT.

20__ _____

20__ _____

20__ _____

20__ _____

20__ _____

March 31

Our focus on mentoring is coming to a close this month. What is your biggest takeaway? How will you apply this in your own life? I invite you to experience Wild Joy through the full experience of mentorship—both mentoring and being mentored—today. Buckle up, because you just may learn something new, empowering, and *transformative* that brings you
—and the world—Joy!

20__ _____

20__ _____

20__ _____

20__ _____

20__ _____

Mrs. Valerie Christina Malicki, MA, LPCC, CPM

At Eve's Joy Professional Mentoring
we specialize in pastoral care for women only.

We offer a unique, world-class blend of faith-based,
therapeutically-informed, certified
professional mentoring.

We would love to hear more about your unique *mentoring vision*, and also provide you with specific *next steps* on how to continue to make it happen.

Simply drop us your current one-sentence *mentoring vision* at EvesJoy.com. You can leave your confidential vision at the bottom of the home page where it says "Leave a message." With this simple entry, you apply to receive one of our periodic, free, confidential, exploration calls. An exploration call is guaranteed to be the best next step toward creating your own unique *mentoring vision*.

Your completely confidential response helps us to create content that further supports you, such as: blogs, emails, webinars, summit/retreat topics, new online groups, podcasts, et cetera.

We are constantly creating new supportive content for you. Please drop us a line and let us know how we can support your next step toward becoming a woman of Wild Joy!

APRIL

Become a Woman of Wild Joy Through *Connecting*.

"What is the sign of a friend? Is it that he tells you his secret sorrows? No, it is that he tells you his secret joys. Many people will confide their secret sorrows to you, but the final mark of intimacy is when they share their secret joys with you."
—Oswald Chambers,
My Utmost for His Highest [14]

Let's visualize your hopes for Joy-Filled connection. Spend 15 minutes imagining your hopes and desires for emotional, mental, spiritual, and physical connection and intimacy. This connection focus might include the connection in any area of your life.

You may want to focus on connection with a new friend, old friends, a common interest group, a spiritual community, or even growth in your relationship with nature through a favorite hiking place, or connection with animals or pets. You may even focus on connecting with a solo hobby or art. This connection may also be a focus on your Divine Connection with God through prayer, worship, and spiritual growth.

---

14. https://www.goodreads.com/work/quotes/1559310-my-utmost-for-his-highest Accessed 9 August 2021.

Next, choose whatever area fits best for you to focus on this month. I recently spent a season focusing on my 17-year love connection with my husband. However, you can focus on love, connection, and relationship in whatever way best fits your own unique life.

What kind of love, connection, and relationship are you looking to focus on, these days? In your wildest dreams, what would this connection look like?

20__ _____

20__ _____

20__ _____

20__ _____

20__ _____

Next, let's expand this vision.
What do you yearn for the connection in your
life to be like this month? What do you want the connection
in your life to be like in five years? Ponder your hopes for
this month, and then, your hopes for five years from now.
Next, imagine actually experiencing all these
hopes you have for connection. Finish
this sentence, today, and each
consecutive year:

This month, I would love for Joy-Filled
connection in my life to look, smell, taste, sound, and feel,
like this:

20__ _____

20__ _____

20__ _____

20__ _____

20__ _____

My long-term, five-year vision for Joy-Filled connection in my life looks, smells, tastes, sounds, and feels, like this:

20__ _____

20__ _____

20__ _____

20__ _____

20__ _____

This is your own unique *connecting vision*. Each day, journal about the lessons you are learning as you continue to expand and create this vision. An easy one-sentence entry for each day is all you need to reflect upon in your journal. Simply write what easily comes to you and enjoy this process of growing in connection.

Remember our mantra this month:

I become a woman of Wild Joy through *connecting*.

April 1

As I explored my own vision of intimacy, I realized that in order for my fantasy to become my reality, I, myself, needed to become the lover and friend I was looking for. Many times, having an amazing relationship starts with you, yourself, being an amazing person.

20__ _____

20__ _____

20__ _____

20__ _____

20__ _____

April 2

As I expanded my vision of all that was possible—and even some things that seemed impossible—little by little, change happened. I made my own personal changes along with this expanded intimacy vision. Every day, I tried to plant good seeds in my relationship that would grow and, one day, blossom. For me, a good place to start was with simple, everyday courtesies. I planted little seeds of picking up my own lunch mess, or working together on meals and schedules. Even today, working together on everyday tasks are just some of the good seeds I still seek to plant regularly, especially in the everyday relationships in my own home.

20__ _____

20__ _____

20__ _____

20__ _____

20__ _____

Mrs. Valerie Christina Malicki, MA, LPCC, CPM

April 3
"Don't judge each day by the harvest
you reap, but by the seeds that you plant."
—Robert Louis Stevenson

20__ _____

20__ _____

20__ _____

20__ _____

20__ _____

April 4

As I continued to expand my own vision of intimacy, I realized that I wanted my marriage to work and my family to stay intact. At first, I wasn't so sure that was possible. We had so many conflicts to work through, it seemed. Yet, this was what I wanted, so it's what I worked for. Every day I continued planting at least a few seeds of teamwork, true intimacy, and everyday courtesies.

20__ _____

20__ _____

20__ _____

20__ _____

20__ _____

Mrs. Valerie Christina Malicki, MA, LPCC, CPM

April 5
What do you want in *your* connection focus that may seem impossible?

20__ _____

20__ _____

20__ _____

20__ _____

20__ _____

April 6
"Vision is the art of seeing the invisible."
—Jonathan Swift

20__ _____

20__ _____

20__ _____

20__ _____

20__ _____

Mrs. Valerie Christina Malicki, MA, LPCC, CPM

April 7

For me, I wanted more of a warm, emotional connection with my husband. After three kids, our connection seemed invisible. For us, it was transformative to work with professional mentors to help us create parts of our relationship that were part of our vision, yet at the time, seemingly invisible. This experience transformed our entire relationship and, ultimately, our family's destiny. It allowed us to "work things out" and thus keep our family intact. Because of this, I am always thankful for professional mentoring. I recommend professional mentoring to any struggling couple or family.

20__ _____

20__ _____

20__ _____

20__ _____

20__ _____

April 8

"Some people believe what they see,
but some people see what they believe."
—Helen Keller

What do you envision and yearn to experience regarding Joy-Filled connection that is currently invisible?

20__ _____

20__ _____

20__ _____

20__ _____

20__ _____

Mrs. Valerie Christina Malicki, MA, LPCC, CPM

April 9

In regards to wanting a warmer, more emotional connection, I began to refocus on what we *did* have. I realized that, yes, we already had a beautiful connection in many ways, in ways I was overlooking in the humdrum of daily life. He was right by my side when all our children were born. In fact, he supported me through the whole labor of our third child, who came quickly and was born right into Daddy's hands at home. In my own frustrations and the stress of having three kids, I was definitely not remembering all his good qualities.

20__ _____

20__ _____

20__ _____

20__ _____

20__ _____

April 10

"...if you are happily married, you are, sad to say, in a minority. It probably means, however, that you have accepted your spouse just the way she is and have not tried to change her in any significant way. I believe this is the key to a successful, long-term marriage."
—J.Bailey Molineux, "The Good Enough Family."[15]

20__ _____

20__ _____

20__ _____

20__ _____

20__ _____

---

15. https://helenair.com/lifestyles/unhappy-marriages-can-be-stable/article_316a30e4-e6af-5632-a8d1-cc7f6861597c.html Accessed 10 July 2022.

Mrs. Valerie Christina Malicki, MA, LPCC, CPM

April 11
In your own experience,
what makes for a good long-term
relationship?

20__ _____

20__ _____

20__ _____

20__ _____

20__ _____

April 12

In my relationship experience, there are many hills, mountains, and valleys along the way to a good relationship. Growing in acceptance of each other has been a challenge, but it has all been worth it. These days, I love the intimacy in my life more and more, and am so glad for the ways our family has worked through challenges together. As it has been said, "We may not have it all together, but together we have it all."

20__ _____

20__ _____

20__ _____

20__ _____

20__ _____

Mrs. Valerie Christina Malicki, MA, LPCC, CPM

April 13

In what ways do you want acceptance to show up in your own vision of connection? Are there any specific ways you desire more acceptance in your relationships?

20__ _____

20__ _____

20__ _____

20__ _____

20__ _____

April 14

For my husband and me, it has been good to continue to work on accepting the "good, bad, and ugly" that is in each of us. The only way to be with the perfect person is to marry a clone. (Haha.) As a friend of mine says, "Vive le difference!" Enjoy and appreciate the differences! For example, I sure appreciate my hubby's good cooking, even though his preference to eat meals later in the day drives me batty at times. I have learned to appreciate the many ways we complement each other. Yes, we have both learned, and continue to learn, to accept each other's differences and utilize them in a way that can work—and actually benefit the whole family.

In order to have more compatibility, what would it look like to give greater acceptance, and even appreciation, for differences?

20__ _____

20__ _____

20__ _____

20__ _____

20__ _____

April 15

"If you want to be average, do what others do. If you want to be AWESOME, do what no one does."
—Alexander Den Heijer

20__ _____

20__ _____

20__ _____

20__ _____

20__ _____

April 16

Do you want to experience an awesome relationship? What is one way, in regards to your relationship, to be different from the masses so your connection can be truly awesome?

20__ _____

20__ _____

20__ _____

20__ _____

20__ _____

April 17

"There is no more powerful motivator in life than joy. It is nearly universally recognized that your brain functions at its best when it is running on the fuel of joy."
—Marcus Warner and Chris Coursey, *The 4 Habits of Joy-Filled Marriages*[16]

20__ _____

20__ _____

20__ _____

20__ _____

20__ _____

---

16. Marcus Warner and Chris Coursey, *The 4 Habits of Joy-Filled Marriages* (Chicago: Northfield Publishing, 2019).

April 18

"When she wakes up, he wakes up. When one partner changes, so does the other. When the student is ready the teacher appears."
—John Gray,
Men Are From Mars, Women Are From Venus [17]

20__ _____

20__ _____

20__ _____

20__ _____

20__ _____

---

17. John Gray, ***Men Are From Mars, Women Are From Venus*** (New York, NY: HarperCollins Publishers, Inc., 1992).

April 19

One way I needed to wake up was to authentically share what I needed in my intimate relationship. I learned positive, inspiring ways to better recognize my own needs and then share them. This made a big difference in the harmony in our relationship. As I shared what I needed, it helped me get what I wanted. (Helloooo!)

20__ _____

20__ _____

20__ _____

20__ _____

20__ _____

April 20

Imagine a world-class relationship mentor is working with you in a private session. Today's session is on recognizing unmet needs and sharing them in your own relationship. How would you describe your own unmet needs in your relationship?

20__ _____

20__ _____

20__ _____

20__ _____

20__ _____

April 21
If your relationship changed to address your unmet needs, what, specifically, would change?

20__ _____

20__ _____

20__ _____

20__ _____

20__ _____

April 22
"A successful relationship has three components: chemistry, compatibility, and communication."
—Patricia Allen

20__ _____

20__ _____

20__ _____

20__ _____

20__ _____

Mrs. Valerie Christina Malicki, MA, LPCC, CPM

April 23
What do you yearn to experience, or what do you already appreciate about the chemistry, compatibility, and/or communication in your life?

20__ _____

20__ _____

20__ _____

20__ _____

20__ _____

April 24

Being compatible when it comes to free time has been a challenge, at times. Especially after kids are in the picture, free time becomes a hot commodity. My husband loves to fish and hunt, press repeat. I love to journal and read after a long country walk. We make sure to come together and find creative ways we can *both* have free time, some to spend together, and some to spend on our own. True, if I were alone, I wouldn't have to deal with anyone else's preferences, but I am glad I get to share life together with my husband. Even with all the ups and downs, togetherness makes the journey of life much more enjoyable.

20__ _____

20__ _____

20__ _____

20__ _____

20__ _____

April 25

In regard to chemistry, many women report that after years of being together, the physical intimacy just gets better and better. I have personally found this to be true. While nothing is ever perfect, these days I am a *happily* married woman. Good, sweet physical intimacy is like perfect icing on a good cake. Experiencing true intimacy with my husband makes the journey of life even sweeter.

20__ _____

20__ _____

20__ _____

20__ _____

20__ _____

April 26
"No journey seems long with a good companion."
—Anonymous

20__

20__

20__

20__

20__

April 27
I invite you to enjoy the love and connection that you have today! What is a fun, exciting, new, adventurous, comforting, or relaxing way to experience Joy in your own relationship today?

20__ _____

20__ _____

20__ _____

20__ _____

20__ _____

April 28
"The only way love
can last a lifetime is if it is unconditional."
—Stephen Kendrick

20__ _____

20__ _____

20__ _____

20__ _____

20__ _____

April 29

"How delicious is your fair beauty; it cannot be described as I count the delights you bring to me. Love has become the greatest. ... The rarest of fruits are found at our doors—the new as well as the old. I have stored them for you, my lover-friend!"
—Song of Solomon 7:6,13b, TPT

20__ _____

20__ _____

20__ _____

20__ _____

20__ _____

April 30

We are coming to a close on our month-long focus on connecting. Let's revisit your vision of Joy-Filled connection together. Imagine you received all you are yearning for in the area of connecting. What would you see, smell, taste, hear, and feel?

20__ _____

20__ _____

20__ _____

20__ _____

20__ _____

Mrs. Valerie Christina Malicki, MA, LPCC, CPM

At Eve's Joy Professional Mentoring
we specialize in pastoral care for women only.

We offer a unique, world-class blend of faith-based, therapeutically-informed, certified professional mentoring.

We would love to hear more about your unique *connecting vision*, and also provide you with specific *next steps* on how to continue to make it happen.

Simply drop us your current one-sentence *connecting vision* at EvesJoy.com. You can leave your confidential vision at the bottom of the home page where it says "Leave a message." With this simple entry, you apply to receive one of our periodic, free, confidential, exploration calls. An exploration call is guaranteed to be the best next step toward creating your own unique *connecting vision.*

Your completely confidential response helps us to create content that further supports you, such as: blogs, emails, webinars, summit/retreat topics, new online groups, podcasts, et cetera.

We are constantly creating new supportive content for you. Please drop us a line and let us know how we can support your next step toward becoming a woman of Wild Joy!

MAY

Become a Woman of Wild Joy
Through *Attaching*.

"The amazing finding that the most powerful predictor of a child's attachment is the coherence of the parent's life narrative allows us to understand how to strengthen our child's attachment to us. We are not destined to repeat the patterns of the past because we can earn our security as an adult by making sense of our life experiences. Making sense of our life stories enables us to have deeper connections with our children, and to live a more joyful and coherent life."
—Daniel J. Siegel, M.D., and Mary Hartzell, M.Ed.,
Parenting From The Inside Out[18]

Imagine living a joyful life of coherence and deep connection, especially in your attachments and relationships. What do you imagine that would be like? Take 15 minutes to ponder what this joyful attachment experience would be like, look like, smell, sound, taste, and feel like. This is our focus for May.

---

18. Daniel J. Seigel, M.D., and Mary Hartzell, M.ED., ***Parenting From The Inside Out: How A Deeper Self-Understanding Can Help You Raise Children Who Thrive*** (New York, New York: Jeremy P. Tarcher/Penguin, a member of Penguin Group (USA) Inc, 2003).

Don't worry, we will unpack this concept all month. Zero overthinking allowed! For now, write what comes to you easily. Let your imagination flow freely. Simply complete the statement below, today and then every consecutive year, in May:

My own unique vision of joyfully attaching in relationships is best described like this:

20__ _____

20__ _____

20__ _____

20__ _____

20__ _____

In May, let's remember our mantra:

I become a woman of Wild Joy through *attaching*.

Mrs. Valerie Christina Malicki, MA, LPCC, CPM

May 1
When you imagine living a life with deep and satisfying connection and attachment, what are the essential parts of your own vision of joyful attachment?

20__ _____

20__ _____

20__ _____

20__ _____

20__ _____

May 2

One essential part of my own vision of attachment is having meaningful, warm, sweet connections at home, in my marriage, and with our children. I so love to snuggle, snuggle, snuggle! Lots of warm, affirming interactions, healthy touch, and good conversation are essential, for me, to experience Wild Joy through attachment.

20__ _____

20__ _____

20__ _____

20__ _____

20__ _____

Mrs. Valerie Christina Malicki, MA, LPCC, CPM

May 3

There have been times when experiencing healthy attachment at home was a huge struggle for me. There have been times when I push people away— even my husband and kids—for deep and also superficial, surface-level reasons. It was good for me to explore at least some of my past relationship styles in order to move forward. I didn't need to take a deep dive every day, but my own process is definitely like peeling an onion—little by little. As I process my emotions in healthy ways, my own behaviors become more healthy. This is the foundation for creating healthy attachments. In this way, the relationships in my home improve
—little by little.

20__ _____

20__ _____

20__ _____

20__ _____

20__ _____

May 4

"Before you have children, you can believe you are a nice person: after you have children you understand how wars start."
—Fay Weldon

20__ _____

20__ _____

20__ _____

20__ _____

20__ _____

May 5

I loved learning in my therapist training program that there are two types of families: those that are dysfunctional, and those that are in denial! Oh my! Yes, it is true that there is no such thing as a "perfect family." And yet, it is so refreshing for me to remember that I am not destined to repeat patterns from the past. With professional help and various avenues of support, I am able to continue learning. We can always be growing and learning new ways to actually experience healthy attachments. In this way, we can transform the attachment patterns in our life and legacy.

20__ _____

20__ _____

20__ _____

20__ _____

20__ _____

May 6

Making sense of my own life story has
helped me have deeper connections with my
kids and—yes—has led to a more
joyful and coherent life.

If we are not destined to repeat patterns
from our past, what attaching pattern do you *not* want to
repeat? For example, my husband grew up with divorced
parents and has decided he wants to do all he can to keep
our family intact.

Instead of repeating old patterns from the
past, how do you want things to be different in
your own life?

20__ _____

20__ _____

20__ _____

20__ _____

20__ _____

May 7

"Children need at least one person in their life who thinks the sun rises and sets on them, who delights in their existence."
—Pamela Leo

20__ _____

20__ _____

20__ _____

20__ _____

20__ _____

May 8

"Treat people as if they were what they ought to be and you help them to become what they are capable of being."
—Johann Wolfgang Von Goethe

20__ _____

20__ _____

20__ _____

20__ _____

20__ _____

May 9

"I was smitten with the idea of making something of myself. But I also wanted my children to have a good time of it. This was a conflict I never resolved as the years passed... It would take a long time for me to understand that I needn't have gone through these shenanigans, that I could have gone to work when the youngest of my children was in high school, or maybe even off to college. But just as the young never really understand, or believe, that there is a long, long time stretching ahead of them in which to do all the things they want, so many mothers like me have felt– and no doubt continue to feel–that if they don't move on the question of career now, the world will simply pass them by."
—Midge Decter, ***An Old Wife's Tale***[19]

20__ _____

20__ _____

20__ _____

20__ _____

20__ _____

---

19. Midge Decter, An Old Wife's Tale: My Seven Decades in Love and War (New York: HarperCollins, 2002).

May 10

Being a mother definitely challenged my ideas and habits. I had been a single career woman for a decade, and was used to doing "what I wanted to do." At times, motherhood brought out my shadow side—that is, a side of me with all my worst qualities. When you consider your own life relationships and attachments, what challenges you? What brings out your "shadow side"?

20__ _____

20__ _____

20__ _____

20__ _____

20__ _____

Mrs. Valerie Christina Malicki, MA, LPCC, CPM

May 11
"Don't you see that children are God's best gift?"
—Psalm 127, TMT

20__ _____

20__ _____

20__ _____

20__ _____

20__ _____

May 12

"'I think the mother's love is the most intense feeling that exists,' she explained. 'And we must talk more about it, we must show it more often in mass media because it can be a cure for all the hate and negativity that surrounds us today.'"
—Miheala Noroc[20]

20__ _____

20__ _____

20__ _____

20__ _____

20__ _____

---

20. https://m.theepochtimes.com/mkt_app/photographer-captures-the-beauty-of-motherhood-from-50-countries-across-the-world-and-its-amazing_3698237.html Accessed 20 August 2022.

May 13

Janet Lynn Salomon, former champion figure skater, wrestled with whether to leave a successful ice-skating career to devote herself to her husband and children.

The following conversation is from an interview:[21]
"What did your friends say when you left your outwardly successful career to be a full-time mother?"
—Nancy Leigh DeMoss, of Revive Our Hearts

"I didn't ask them."
—Janet Lynn Salomon *(emphasis mine)*

20__ _____

20__ _____

20__ _____

20__ _____

20__ _____

---

21. https://www.reviveourhearts.com/podcast/revive-our-hearts/season/metamorphosis-of-a-mom-with-janet-lynn/ Accessed 30 January 2022.

May 14

"An honest answer is like a kiss on the lips."
—Proverbs 24:26, NIV

20__ _____

20__ _____

20__ _____

20__ _____

20__ _____

Mrs. Valerie Christina Malicki, MA, LPCC, CPM

May 15

"We have seen in study after study that compulsive positive thinkers are more likely to develop disease and less likely to survive. Genuine positive thinking—or, more deeply, positive being—empowers us to know that we have nothing to fear from truth. 'Health is not just a matter of thinking happy thoughts,' writes the molecular researcher Candace Pert. 'Sometimes the biggest impetus to healing can come from jump-starting the immune system with a burst of long-suppressed anger.'"
—Gabor Maté, ***When the Body Says No: The Cost of Hidden Stress***[22]

20__ _____

20__ _____

20__ _____

20__ _____

20__ _____

---

[22]. https://www.goodreads.com/book/show/450534.When_the_Body_Says_No Accessed 29 January 2022.

May 16
When you were growing up, were you allowed to be angry and still be confident you were loved, unconditionally?

20__ _____

20__ _____

20__ _____

20__ _____

20__ _____

Mrs. Valerie Christina Malicki, MA, LPCC, CPM

May 17

It can be challenging to express any kind of emotion, especially if we were not taught or given a good model of how to do so in a healthy way. Learning how to identify and express anger—and all emotions—has been a process in my own journey.

Before we can be interdependent and have healthy attachments, we must first be able to be independent. Being independent includes very simply being responsible for our own emotions and our own lives. What are healthy ways you can identify, express, and be responsible for your own emotions?

(If you are struggling to find healthy ways to express your emotions, you may explore seeking professional support. Identifying and expressing emotions is critical to mental health.)

20__ _____

20__ _____

20__ _____

20__ _____

20__ _____

May 18

"She's the sort of woman who lives for others—you can tell the others by their hunted expression."
—C.S. Lewis, ***The Screwtape Letters***[23]

20__ _____

20__ _____

20__ _____

20__ _____

20__ _____

---

23. https://www.goodreads.com/work/quotes/2920952-the-screwtape-letters Accessed 29 January 2022.

Mrs. Valerie Christina Malicki, MA, LPCC, CPM

May 19

Many times, those who "live for others" simply have not found ways to experience healthy independence. It makes for the healthiest and most mutually satisfying relationships when we are able to express love in ways that are not controlling or suffocating. Healthy relationships arise from many things, including healthy expression and ownership of feelings. What would it look like for you to take total responsibility for your own healthy emotional expression—and even your life? How would this be a wonderful way to truly love another?

20__ _____

20__ _____

20__ _____

20__ _____

20__ _____

May 20

"A house is built of logs and stone,
Of tiles and posts and piers.
A home is built of loving deeds
That stand a thousand years."
—Victor Hugo

20__ _____

20__ _____

20__ _____

20__ _____

20__ _____

Mrs. Valerie Christina Malicki, MA, LPCC, CPM

May 21
How would having total responsibility for your own life, and building healthy attachments with loving *deeds*, impact your life—and the legacy you pass on to the next generation?

20__ _____

20__ _____

20__ _____

20__ _____

20__ _____

May 22

"Few things in this world are as important as raising children. In every age, every era, every time and place, children are our treasures, our future, our immortality—the vital link in the chain of humanity."
—William Martin, ***The Parent's Tao Te Ching: Ancient Advice for Modern Parents***[24]

20__ _____

20__ _____

20__ _____

20__ _____

20__ _____

---

24. https://www.goodreads.com/work/quotes/98167-the-parent-s-tao-te-ching-ancient-advice-for-modern-parents-a-new-int. Accessed 30 January 2022.

May 23
"The hand that rocks the cradle rules the world."
—Anonymous

20__ _____

20__ _____

20__ _____

20__ _____

20__ _____

May 24
"An ounce of mother is worth a pound of clergy."
—Spanish Proverb

20__ _____

20__ _____

20__ _____

20__ _____

20__ _____

Mrs. Valerie Christina Malicki, MA, LPCC, CPM

May 25

"Treasure each moment, each stage, each season of life. Be thankful for your children continually. They are a precious gift. It gets easier. The children grow so quickly, and soon they will be out on their own."
—Summer Bixler, Joy-Filled
Wife and Mother of 10 Blessings

20__ _____

20__ _____

20__ _____

20__ _____

20__ _____

May 26

"Give me just one generation
of youth, and I'll transform the whole world."
—Vladimir Ilyich Lenin

20__ _____

20__ _____

20__ _____

20__ _____

20__ _____

Mrs. Valerie Christina Malicki, MA, LPCC, CPM

May 27
"A truly rich man is one whose children run into his arms when his hands are empty."
—Anonymous

20__ _____

20__ _____

20__ _____

20__ _____

20__ _____

May 28

"'Sometimes,' said Pooh,
'the smallest things take up the most
room in your heart.'"
—A.A. Milne

20__ _____

20__ _____

20__ _____

20__ _____

20__ _____

Mrs. Valerie Christina Malicki, MA, LPCC, CPM

May 29

Ultimately, my strongest and most secure attachment is with God. I know God loves me and always will. I make lots of mistakes as a wife, parent, friend, and human being. Yet, God accepts me, and guides me, and loves me unconditionally, always. My relationship with my own kids is the same. No matter the mistakes of my children, I always love them. Being a parent has taught me big lessons on unconditional love. No matter what, I will always love my children. God's Love for us must be at least as lavish and unwavering as my own feeble and flawed efforts in expressing love to my children. God is the perfect, most loving parent imaginable to His children.

20__ _____

20__ _____

20__ _____

20__ _____

20__ _____

May 30

"God is bedrock under my feet, the
castle in which I live, my rescuing knight. My God
—the high crag where I run for dear life, hiding behind the
boulders, safe in the granite hideout; my mountaintop refuge,
he saves me from ruthless men. But me he caught—reached
all the way from sky to sea; he pulled me out of that ocean of
hate, that enemy chaos, the void in which I was drowning.
They hit me when I was down, but God stuck by me.
He stood me up on a wide-open field;
I stood there saved
—surprised to be loved!"
—2 Samuel 22:2-5, TMT

20__ _____

20__ _____

20__ _____

20__ _____

20__ _____

Mrs. Valerie Christina Malicki, MA, LPCC, CPM

May 31

Let's reimagine your own vision of joyful attachment. When you imagine living a life with deep and satisfying connection and attachment, now, what are the essential parts of your own *expanded* vision of joyful attachment?

I invite you to experience Wild Joy today, through attaching.

Enjoy—and savor—all your sweet, precious moments!

20__ _____

20__ _____

20__ _____

20__ _____

20__ _____

At Eve's Joy Professional Mentoring
we specialize in pastoral care for women only.

We offer a unique, world-class blend of
faith-based, therapeutically-informed, certified
professional mentoring.

We would love to hear more about your unique *joyful attachment vision*, and also provide you with specific *next steps* on how to continue to make it happen.

Simply drop us your current one-sentence *joyful attachment vision* at EvesJoy.com. You can leave your confidential vision at the bottom of the home page where it says "Leave a message." With this simple entry, you apply to receive one of our periodic, free, confidential, exploration calls. An exploration call is guaranteed to be the best next step toward creating your own unique *joyful attachment vision*.

Your completely confidential response helps us to create content that further supports you, such as: blogs, emails, webinars, summit/retreat topics, new online groups, podcasts, et cetera.

We are constantly creating new supportive content for you. Please drop us a line, and let us know how we can support your next step toward becoming a woman of Wild Joy!

JUNE

Become a Woman of Wild Joy Through *Working*.

"Work with all your might, but never trust in your work. Pray with all your might for the blessing of God, but work at the same time with all diligence, with all patience, with all perseverance. Pray, then, and work. Work and pray. And still again pray, and then work. And so on, all the days of your life. The result will surely be abundant blessing. Whether you see much fruit or little fruit, such kind of service will be blessed."
—George Müller[25]

Spend 15 minutes visualizing what you imagine to be your ideal "great work" in this world. A great work is the work that you came here to do. Your great work is a part of your destiny. I feel God made me to be the matriarch of my tribe, to be a wife and mom and visionary woman. Every person has a "great work" mission in life.

Imagine what six (or fewer) words would be on your grave, or the theme of your eulogy. Those words contain your great work. It may be a certain, specific title or task, but more likely it has nothing to do with things like a circumstance or position. Just ponder whatever words come easily to your heart and mind.

---

25. https://www.georgemuller.org/quotes/the-great-secret-of-success Accessed 11 December 2021.

You may wish for your own life to
best be described as something like this:

- "She brought the world Joy"
- "Beloved grandmother, wife, friend"
- "Blessed Matriarch"
- "Friend of God, Friend to All"
- "Wise Leader. Loving Mom. Godly Example."
- "She led by love and example"
- "Writer, Thinker, Prayer, Lover, Leader, Friend"
- "Healer, Helper, Friend, Warrior for Good"
- "Cherished leader, lover, a light"
- "Blessed, Beloved Mama Bear To All"
- "Joyful Wife, Mom, Friend"
- "Adventurous, Inspiring, Kind Woman of Faith"
- "Homeschool Mom, Loving Wife, Prayer Warrior"

Mrs. Valerie Christina Malicki, MA, LPCC, CPM

When I pass on to heaven,
I would love my own gravestone to read:
"Blessed, Joyful Wife, Mother, Sister, Friend"

Every year as you return to this month, simply repeat these reflections, and write a reflection that fits well for that year. You may find your vision to be the same, or that it may change. I love to explore my own growth. Sometimes there are big changes, and sometimes there are unchanging, consistent themes. There are no right or wrong answers here, just reflections. It can be interesting, fun, and powerful to reflect. This is all about increasing
one's awareness and insight.

Let's document together what is current
for you, now. Each consecutive year, as you return to this exercise, write your answer, below.

Becoming a Woman of Wild Joy

"This year, I imagine my
gravestone inscription to be like this:"

20__ _____

20__ _____

20__ _____

20__ _____

20__ _____

With our monthly focus in place, we are all set to dive into our daily reflections. Remember our mantra this month:

**I become a woman of Wild Joy
through *working*.**

Mrs. Valerie Christina Malicki, MA, LPCC, CPM

June 1

As I imagine my own great work vision, I imagine a family gathering with all my children and even grandchildren. We are giggling and playing by (and in) a refreshing pond. The summer sun sets in the pink sky. The bullfrogs bellow and charm us with their harmonies. We eat blueberries and ice cream and drink sweet tea. We are making another new sweet memory. Together, we share conversation, unplug, play, and enjoy a summer holiday weekend. This is all part of my own "great work" vision.

Let's describe your "great work" vision.
How does it feel, smell, taste, sound, and look, today?

20__ _____

20__ _____

20__ _____

20__ _____

20__ _____

June 2

"Your gifts lie in the place where your values, passions...strengths meet. Discovering that place is the first step toward sculpting your masterpiece, Your Life."
—Michelangelo

Have you ever considered your life to be a masterpiece? Let's imagine this month that the *work* you are doing is like sculpting a beautiful masterpiece. The beautiful masterpiece we are
working on is your life!

20__ _____

20__ _____

20__ _____

20__ _____

20__ _____

Mrs. Valerie Christina Malicki, MA, LPCC, CPM

June 3

When it comes to the "great work" vision, it is rightly named, as there really is so much work, work, work involved. There are always "busywork" tasks to be finished. Often, "busywork" is urgent and definitely necessary, to a point, but not always super important in the grand scheme of life.

Busywork includes "the daily grind" of accomplishing the day's regular tasks. My own busywork is the steady stream of dishes, laundry, meals, homeschooling lessons, groceries, bills, and errands—*press repeat*. All this needs to happen, but I don't want my gravestone to say, "Her laundry was so well done!"

What is your busywork?

20__ _____

20__ _____

20__ _____

20__ _____

20__ _____

June 4
"Everything is hard before it is easy."
— J. W. Goethe

20__ _____

20__ _____

20__ _____

20__ _____

20__ _____

Mrs. Valerie Christina Malicki, MA, LPCC, CPM

June 5

I feel like this "hard, then easy" experience is my own experience with doing laundry for an active, adventurous, country-living family of six. These days, I feel like I would be able to do laundry in my sleep. (Actually, when each of the four children were little babies, many days I was like a sleep-deprived zombie. So…doing laundry in my sleep was exactly what I did!)

Think about a time that you experienced a task being oh-so-hard at first. Then, over time, remember how it became so easy, that it was truly like a walk in the park. How has this experience occurred for you?

20__ _____

20__ _____

20__ _____

20__ _____

20__ _____

June 6
"If you are going through hell, keep going."
—Winston Churchill

20__ _____

20__ _____

20__ _____

20__ _____

20__ _____

June 7

When in the overwhelm of busywork,
I must conscientiously choose to *keep going*. I must find
ways to continue, to *move forward*. One
way I tackle busywork is with the
"15-minute-get-started-rule."

I set a timer and do focused work
for 15 minutes. This 15 minute choice gets me moving on
a busywork task—whether it be working on homeschooling
lessons, tackling financial planning, organizing socks, or
clearing clutter. After 15 minutes, I can quit. Sometimes
I do, but often the 15 minutes just gets me going. Many
times, I quickly have an hour of focused, productive
busywork completed. Whew! Yay!

20__ _____

20__ _____

20__ _____

20__ _____

20__ _____

June 8

Developing 15-minute habits can be more effective than it may seem...at first. Plus, 15-minute habits are a super easy way to get started.

What is one, new, 15-minute habit that would make a significant, leveraged impact in your day?

How will you make a way to practice this new habit every day, for the rest of this month?

20__ _____

20__ _____

20__ _____

20__ _____

20__ _____

Mrs. Valerie Christina Malicki, MA, LPCC, CPM

June 9

As I consider my own *great work* vision,
I am often overwhelmed. One way I relieve my stress is by writing down—on paper or on a device—my intentions, goals, and necessary work. Anything I write down—either on paper or online—becomes more manageable... and then, more possible.

What is an area of your work that
would benefit from its details being written down?

20__ _____

20__ _____

20__ _____

20__ _____

20__ _____

June 10

When I write down all my necessary work tasks, I use planners, simple to-do lists, habit trackers, or even guided journals specific to the needed topic. Guided journals can focus on various areas of life, such as: goal achievement, processing emotions, financial planning, or productivity. Becoming more effective in a specific area helps my overall life to be more effective, and even more satisfying —like a positive domino effect.

As you have worked toward success in one area of your life, how has it caused even more success in other areas of your life?

20__ _____

20__ _____

20__ _____

20__ _____

20__ _____

Mrs. Valerie Christina Malicki, MA, LPCC, CPM

June 11

When I am able to experience success with my never-ending cycles of groceries, cleaning, homeschooling, bedtimes, etc, it opens up more time for visionary work. Think of visionary work as **the work that incorporates what you _do_ want on your gravestone inscription.**

Visionary work may involve building strong relationships, setting high goals, creating a strong family legacy of love, having solid and regular prayer time, or just *creating* for the sheer pleasure of sharing your creative gifts with the world.

What visionary work feels most important to you right now?

20__ _____

20__ _____

20__ _____

20__ _____

20__ _____

June 12
"If you want to change the world, go home and love your family."
—Mother Teresa

20__ _____

20__ _____

20__ _____

20__ _____

20__ _____

Mrs. Valerie Christina Malicki, MA, LPCC, CPM

June 13

Mother Teresa's quote about loving your family at home is a practical example of visionary work. It requires vision to step back from all the rigors of daily busywork and the personas of public image, and be intentional about loving your family at home. This type of work is not urgent, but is one example of work that may be vitally important to one's own "great work" vision.

What kind of visionary work is vital, yet not urgent, to your own *great work* vision?

20__ _____

20__ _____

20__ _____

20__ _____

20__ _____

June 14

Visionary work can encompass the work of investing time, energy, and resources in one's growth, development, life direction, and dreams. This growth may be: financial, intellectual, spiritual, physical, relational, emotional, mental, or any growth that aligns with your own unique vision. Visionary work is work that is vital regarding one's life mission. Yet, since this work is not urgent, it often gets put on the "back burner."

Ponder time in your own life spent on visionary work, such as: building relationships, planning, imagining, aligning, spiritual growth, brainstorming, praying, rejuvenating, resting, exercising, visualizing possibilities, emotional healing, etc. Anything that is truly important, yet not urgent. What is something you have put on the "back burner," yet deep down, you know it needs your attention?

20__ _____

20__ _____

20__ _____

20__ _____

20__ _____

Mrs. Valerie Christina Malicki, MA, LPCC, CPM

June 15

I invite you to "do the work" toward your own growth, and to actually *do your vital visionary work.* Will you invest your time to create strong relationships, spend time in prayer, set long-term goals, or even dream of saying "YES," to an out-of-the-box opportunity? Will you journal about a long-term wild dream, or spend time on a long walk? What is one way you will take time for your own non-urgent, but vitally important, visionary work, today?

20__ _____

20__ _____

20__ _____

20__ _____

20__ _____

June 16

As my own vision expanded, my energies became more focused. I realized I needed to cut out a lot of situations and commitments that simply did not align with my great work. It takes one thousand "NOs" to say "YES" from deep within. Saying "YES" from deep within is saying "YES" to the vision of your own unique "great work."

20__ _____

20__ _____

20__ _____

20__ _____

20__ _____

June 17

"I saw the angel in the marble and carved until I set him free."
—Michelangelo

20__ _____

20__ _____

20__ _____

20__ _____

20__ _____

June 18

I invite you to ponder "setting free" the masterpiece that is your own life. Do you need to "carve away" negative emotions, self-sabotaging behaviors, or a bad habit that has become a destructive addiction? As you consider the masterpiece work of your life, what needs to be carved away?

20__ _____

20__ _____

20__ _____

20__ _____

20__ _____

Mrs. Valerie Christina Malicki, MA, LPCC, CPM

June 19

The vision of my own great work, at times, felt like climbing a giant mountain. At other times, it felt like climbing a giant mountain with a huge boulder on my back. At times, it all felt so hard! I needed to have faith. I needed to have faith that this steep climb before me was even possible. As they say, *faith over fear!* This motto has been a positive focus for me as I continue on with my "great work" vision.

How will you show *faith over fear*, today?

20__ _____

20__ _____

20__ _____

20__ _____

20__ _____

June 20

"I tell you the truth, if you have faith as small as a mustard seed you can say to this mountain, 'Move from here to there' and it will move. Nothing will be impossible for you."
—Matthew 17:20, NIV

As you ponder your own great work, does it ever feel like a mountain? Why or why not?

20__ _____

20__ _____

20__ _____

20__ _____

20__ _____

Mrs. Valerie Christina Malicki, MA, LPCC, CPM

June 21

My mother, Linda Gore Smith, wore a mustard-seed necklace. It always reminded her—and me—of yesterday's verse. With faith, nothing is impossible. In this way, my mom's example of faith was one part of her own "great work," which was the passing on of a faith legacy.

What is one life lesson that you want to pass to the next generation?

20__ _____

20__ _____

20__ _____

20__ _____

20__ _____

June 22

"These mountains that you are carrying, you were only supposed to climb."
—Najwa Zebia, Author of *Mind Platter*[26]

20__ _____

20__ _____

20__ _____

20__ _____

20__ _____

---

26. https://quotesberry.com/these-mountains-that-you-are-carrying-you-were-only-supposed-climb-najwa-zebia/ Accessed 7 June 2022.

Mrs. Valerie Christina Malicki, MA, LPCC, CPM

June 23

My mother's legacy includes the life lesson of strong determination, regarding both work and life in general. Mom had a motto about determination: "Where there's a will, there's a way." My mom also emulated this determination in her faith, marriage, family, and life.

As a longtime family friend shared recently with me, "Your mother was a force!"

20__ _____

20__ _____

20__ _____

20__ _____

20__ _____

June 24
One life CAN make a large impact!

How are doing with developing habits that
allow your own life to have an intentional impact?

20__ _____

20__ _____

20__ _____

20__ _____

20__ _____

Mrs. Valerie Christina Malicki, MA, LPCC, CPM

June 25

"Believe in what you want so much
that it has no choice but to materialize."
—Anonymous

What small step of success will help you,
today, to focus on having "the will" to make "a way" for
doing the work of your great work vision?

20__ _____

20__ _____

20__ _____

20__ _____

20__ _____

June 26

Let's imagine a new, *expanded* "great work" vision. I invite you to dream big, and I challenge you to increase your vision by ten times, and then by a hundred times. As you imagine your *expanded* "great work" vision, what are you hearing, smelling, tasting, feeling, and seeing, today?

20__ _____

20__ _____

20__ _____

20__ _____

20__ _____

Mrs. Valerie Christina Malicki, MA, LPCC, CPM

June 27
"Be strong and courageous for
your work will be rewarded!"
—2 Chronicles 15:7, NLT

How are you doing with the new,
15-minute work habit that you began earlier this month?

What is one reward, positive benefit,
or good experience that has been the result
of your commitment?

20__ _____

20__ _____

20__ _____

20__ _____

20__ _____

June 28

"The secret of joy in work is contained in one word: excellence. To know how to do something well is to enjoy it."
—Pearl S. Buck

20__ _____

20__ _____

20__ _____

20__ _____

20__ _____

Mrs. Valerie Christina Malicki, MA, LPCC, CPM

June 29

Brave friend, I invite you to experience the secret joy of practicing excellence in *all* your work. I invite you to learn, and keep learning, to do your work *well*. I invite you to learn to do your work so *well* that you ENJOY it!

Okay, friend…
Ready…Set…DO THE WORK TODAY!

What MUST you DO today?
(Bonus points if it is *visionary* work!)

20__ _____

20__ _____

20__ _____

20__ _____

20__ _____

June 30

As we come to a close this month, let's reflect on this month's focus: *working* on sculpting a beautiful masterpiece, the masterpiece of your life. Today, as you reflect on experiencing Wild Joy through working, what is the most essential lesson you are learning?

20__ _____

20__ _____

20__ _____

20__ _____

20__ _____

Mrs. Valerie Christina Malicki, MA, LPCC, CPM

At Eve's Joy Professional Mentoring
we specialize in pastoral care for women only.

We offer a unique, world-class blend of
faith-based, therapeutically-informed, certified
professional mentoring.

We would love to hear more about your unique
working vision, and also provide you with specific next
steps on how to continue to make it happen.

Simply drop us your current one-sentence
working vision at EvesJoy.com. You can leave your
confidential vision at the bottom of the home page where it
says "Leave a message." With this simple entry, you apply
to receive one of our periodic, free, confidential, exploration
calls. An exploration call is guaranteed to be the best
next step toward creating your own
unique *working vision*.

Your completely confidential response helps
us to create content that further supports you, such as:
blogs, emails, webinars, summit/retreat topics, new
online groups, podcasts, et cetera.

We are constantly creating new supportive
content for you. Please drop us a line and let us know
how we can support your next step toward becoming
a woman of Wild Joy!

JULY

Become A Woman Of Wild Joy
Through *Repairing*.

"The Spirit of God, the Master, is on me because God anointed me. He sent me to preach good news to the poor, heal the heartbroken, Announce freedom to all captives, pardon all prisoners. God sent me to announce the year of his grace—a celebration of God's destruction of our enemies—and to comfort all who mourn, To care for the needs of all who mourn in Zion, give them bouquets of roses instead of ashes, Messages of joy instead of news of doom, a praising heart instead of a languid spirit. Rename them 'Oaks of Righteousness' planted by God to display his glory. They'll rebuild the old ruins, raise a new city out of the wreckage. They'll start over on the ruined cities, take the rubble left behind and make it new. You'll hire outsiders to herd your flocks and foreigners to work your fields, But you'll have the title 'Priests of God,' honored as ministers of our God. You'll feast on the bounty of nations, you'll bask in their glory. Because you got a double dose of trouble and more than your share of contempt, Your inheritance in the land will be doubled and your joy go on forever."
—Isaiah 61:1-7, TMT

Over the years, as I journal, I see themes, issues, and victories being recorded, and I know that yes, I am doing the work of repair. By God's Grace, as I gain clarity and do this repair work, the "straw" of my life transforms into gold. This gold repairs all my broken places—as in the Japanese art of kintsugi. In this magnificent art, pots are repaired with gold, and they are incredibly more beautiful for having been broken. By God's Grace, this is my entire life—repaired with gold.

When my husband and I had our third child, we were on cloud nine for a lot of obvious and wonderful reasons. My son was caught by Daddy at birth. His actual birth occurred as an unplanned (and super exhilarating) home birth! My first and only son was born naturally quick, literally 12 minutes after I called my midwife. He was born fabulously perfect. Best of all, he arrived so smoothly. (The best day of my life!) Yet, what comes up must go down—or so they say. Several months later, our decade-long relationship hit absolute rock bottom. (Some of the worst days of my life, as I was terribly worn-out in all ways, sleep-deprived, and, well, there was a lot of fighting. Ugh!) Through lots of helpful circumstances, professional mentors, personal mentors, Divine intervention, and answered prayers, we began to repair our relationship. The process for us could be described as: crisis to catharsis to connection. So that is my own (very, very short version) of how I have repaired something in my life with gold.

Let's re-focus on your chosen repair area.

Mrs. Valerie Christina Malicki, MA, LPCC, CPM

What needs repair for you this month? Is it a recent stressful issue, scheduling/time management problem, or even an area of burnout for you? Would you like to repair your finances, your relationship with God, your relationship with others, your vision of your purpose, your health, or your commitment to experiencing personal growth? I invite you to choose an area where you would love to transform brokenness, struggle, or difficulty into gold. This is any area in your personal, interpersonal, or professional life where you yearn to experience repair and transformation.

How would it be to gain clarity, do the work and "make repairs with gold?" How would it be to, first, imagine this "broken" area repaired with gold? Any area in which you would love to experience change is perfect for this month's focus.

Imagine this broken area is now beautiful, just like Japanese pottery that is repaired with gold. In this renewed, "repaired with gold" experience, what are you smelling, hearing, tasting, feeling, and seeing? Simply ponder what comes to you now.

We will continue to expand on your *"repairing with gold"* vision. Simply write your answers today, and then each consecutive year.

The area right now that most
feels in need of repairing with gold is this:

20__ _____

20__ _____

20__ _____

20__ _____

20__ _____

In five years, I would love for this
area to be totally transformed, and to be like this:

20__ _____

20__ _____

20__ _____

20__ _____

20__ _____

This is our repairing with gold vision and
focus for July. Remember our mantra this month:

**I become a woman of Wild Joy
through repairing.**

Mrs. Valerie Christina Malicki, MA, LPCC, CPM

July 1

Before I began repairing my life, I needed to feel the pain. That may sound odd, but scar tissue doesn't have much feeling sometimes. Pain needs to be felt. Pain, much like a hand to the stove, can signal a person to make a positive change.

20__ _____

20__ _____

20__ _____

20__ _____

20__ _____

July 2

As we begin this month of repair, just BE for 15 minutes. BE. BE still. BE quiet. Ask God to open your heart to the repair work of healing. Ask Him, who knows all, to show *you* what needs to be repaired. Where are you feeling pain in life? This is often a place to start as we begin our month of focusing on repair.

20__ _____

20__ _____

20__ _____

20__ _____

20__ _____

July 3

Areas we feel pain may be referred to as areas where we are "cursed." In my experiences of working with emotional needs and mental health, I have found we often carry wounds we are not even aware of. We are humans, mere mortals, who live in a very imperfect world. We all have emotional wounds to some degree. *Repairing* emotional wounds is somewhat like resetting a bone broken long ago. It can be painful, for a time, to re-break a bone in order to reset it correctly, but that pain is worth it. Healing and setting things right makes it all worth it. There is a sacredness about revisiting painful places in our lives. I found I needed to experience a lot of compassion for myself as I began this journey.

20__ _____

20__ _____

20__ _____

20__ _____

20__ _____

July 4

Extra tender loving care (TLC) is needed to face difficult changes and profound healing experiences. What would it look like to give yourself some extra TLC as you embark on this month of repairing? How would you show some kindness to yourself as you prepare for the task of repairing with gold? What kind of TLC does your body, mind, and spirit need the most today?

20__ _____

20__ _____

20__ _____

20__ _____

20__ _____

Mrs. Valerie Christina Malicki, MA, LPCC, CPM

July 5

For me, showing myself love and kindness means showing myself the same love and kindness I would offer a hurt child who is in my care. How could you offer yourself the love and kindness that you show to others?

20__ _____

20__ _____

20__ _____

20__ _____

20__ _____

July 6

At times, it is essential to turn my concern for others away, and turn toward my own essential repair work. As I prepare for my healing and repair work, I am sure to give my body, mind, and soul some extra TLC. I may sleep in, or I may splurge on a fun playful time, or celebration time, instead of working around the clock. I may give myself a "mental health day" to unplug and slow down, et cetera. What extra TLC does your body, mind, and spirit most need on this day?

20__ _____

20__ _____

20__ _____

20__ _____

20__ _____

July 7

"Every woman who heals herself
helps heal all the women who came before her,
and all those who come after her."
—Dr. Christiane Northrup

20__ _____

20__ _____

20__ _____

20__ _____

20__ _____

July 8

"I will surely bless you and make
your descendants as numerous as the stars in the sky and
as the sand on the seashore."
—Genesis 22:17a, NIV

20__ _____

20__ _____

20__ _____

20__ _____

20__ _____

Mrs. Valerie Christina Malicki, MA, LPCC, CPM

July 9

As I yearned to experience Wild Joy, I knew God was speaking to me about repairing my wounds. Some wounds were generations deep. The generational curses would end with me. I would begin a new legacy of blessing.

20__ _____

20__ _____

20__ _____

20__ _____

20__ _____

July 10

One area of repair in my own life was repairing the grief and trauma of "the accident," as some family members call it. I suddenly lost my mom when I was in college. She died instantly in a tragic car accident when she was only 42. My nephew died in the wreck, too. My sister was in the passenger seat, but survived with little physical injury. Her severe trauma was largely unrecognized until her own untimely death, from cancer, at age 37. All these wounds cut me to the core, and altered the course of my entire life.

What would you describe as a life event or circumstance that cut you to the core?

20__ _____

20__ _____

20__ _____

20__ _____

20__ _____

Mrs. Valerie Christina Malicki, MA, LPCC, CPM

July 11

"When you remember me...even after I die, you can still see my face and hear my voice and speak to me in your heart."
—Frederick Buechner

20__ _____

20__ _____

20__ _____

20__ _____

20__ _____

July 12

I remember my mom's robust determination: in her lifelong, loving marriage to my dad, in her lifelong commitment to her four loved children, in her warmth and kind heart for other people, in her entire personal life, and in so many places and spaces where her large influence was present. Robust determination is definitely a part of my own mother's legacy. All those fond memories, and even some difficult moments, bring a smile to my face these days. (Like how we said her blueish-green eyes went straight green when she was mad!) In recalling all these memories, I experience *repair*.

20__ _____

20__ _____

20__ _____

20__ _____

20__ _____

Mrs. Valerie Christina Malicki, MA, LPCC, CPM

July 13

As I have birthed my own children, now,
I have focused on passing on the positive life lessons given to me from my mother. I feel within me a sense of generational repair in being a mother. I am a mother of four children, as my own mother was. It's almost impossible to explain, but I experience healing, too, in my own experience of motherhood. I feel Mom cheering me on in the heavens. Again, this is impossible to explain, but it is so real in my heart.

Have you ever experienced a sense
of repair, even in the midst of painful experiences? Why or why not?

20__ _____

20__ _____

20__ _____

20__ _____

20__ _____

July 14

I hope and pray I get the chance to enjoy parts of life on this earth that my own mother did not. I want to experience becoming a grandmother, and so many more of life's milestones—like seeing the weddings and achievements of my children. I hope to enjoy the quiet bliss and mixed feelings of a home that is, at times, like an "empty nest." I hope to experience the later, golden years of contentment and deepened intimacy with my husband in our emptier nest. I hope for the rest of my life to be the best of my life!

20__ _____

20__ _____

20__ _____

20__ _____

20__ _____

Mrs. Valerie Christina Malicki, MA, LPCC, CPM

July 15

Ironically, in losing my own mother —and now, in experiencing becoming a mother myself—I do feel a sense of repair, and even completion. For me, that completion is in becoming a woman who carries on a beautiful legacy. This beautiful legacy began even before my own mother. I feel in my heart profound Wild Joy in being able to pass on the beautiful legacy of all my foremothers. I feel repair in creating an example and a life of Wild Joy. The next generation of women in my family will also continue to repair our legacy with gold—even more so than I have. This is my prayer, as I lead the way. As generational wounds are repaired, I continue to be a wounded healer. Creating a healthy family legacy is a profound experience. It can be a rather mysterious, Joy-Filled experience. Mysteriously, I do experience immense Wild Joy in being a part of generational *repair*.

20__ _____

20__ _____

20__ _____

20__ _____

20__ _____

July 16

Let's explore aspects of your own history or circumstances. When you think about areas that need repair, what comes up for you? What feels broken? Often, these are the whispers that we try—sometimes desperately—to drown out with all sorts of things. Even good things like charity work can sometimes be attempts to drown out these whispers.

Ask yourself: in what area do *I most yearn for transformation*? Your answer may be: mental health, social health, financial health, physical health, or spiritual health, or any area of life that yearns for change. This answer is often related to what needs to be *repaired* the most.

20__ _____

20__ _____

20__ _____

20__ _____

20__ _____

July 17

There have been times my interpersonal relationships have felt broken and in need of repair. I need a lot of safety and reassurance at times. With one small phone call about my mom's sudden car accident, my whole world came crashing down. Trust me, a tragedy like that puts you on red alert for security and safety, especially in relationships.

What are "danger signals," triggers, frustrations, or stresses, for you? All of these experiences can be whispers that show you there is a need for repair work in an area of your life.

20__ _____

20__ _____

20__ _____

20__ _____

20__ _____

July 18

"Being able to feel safe with other people is probably the single most important aspect of mental health; safe connections are fundamental to meaningful and satisfying lives."
—Bessel A. van der Kolk[27]

20__ _____

20__ _____

20__ _____

20__ _____

20__ _____

---

27. https://www.besselvanderkolk.com/ Accessed 28 January 2022.

Mrs. Valerie Christina Malicki, MA, LPCC, CPM

July 19
"To the world you may be one person,
but to one person you may be the world."
—Anonymous

20__ _____

20__ _____

20__ _____

20__ _____

20__ _____

July 20

"The people who influence us most are not those who buttonhole us and talk to us, but those who live their lives like the stars in heaven and the lilies in the field, perfectly simply and unaffectedly. Those are the lives that mould."
—Oswald Chambers,
My Utmost for His Highest[28]

20__ _____

20__ _____

20__ _____

20__ _____

20__ _____

---

28. https://www.goodreads.com/quotes/259990-the-people-who-influence-us-most-are-not-those-who Accessed 23 April 2022.

Mrs. Valerie Christina Malicki, MA, LPCC, CPM

July 21

I have found that those who most influenced my own repair and healing of emotional wounds were exactly the people who lived simply and unaffectedly—and kindly. Oh, so kindly! I thank God for the humongous community of those who come around me when I experience the pains of grief or tragedy. It is strange how one can feel so powerfully loved and supported, yet all alone at the same time. That's how I often feel in my wounded places
and in times of loss.

20__ _____

20__ _____

20__ _____

20__ _____

20__ _____

July 22

When you consider painful experiences
(and even, possibly, generations-deep pain) from
dysfunctional relationships, abuse, addiction, or a myriad
of places, what feelings arise? Anger? Rage? Numbness?
Apathy toward these experiences you wish didn't exist?
A feeling of possible sadness, or fear that something may
happen again? Whatever the feeling, it is
healthy to *express* your feelings.

There is a common saying about how it is
good to "get your feelings out." This is like a teapot letting
off steam. And, this saying is true. Letting pressure out is
far better than pretending the heat and pressure are not
there. Keeping it in may work, for a time, until there is an
explosion. What sort of emotional steam do you need to let
out today? I invite you to express your feelings in
safe places today.

(Your journal is a perfect place to start!)

20__ _____

20__ _____

20__ _____

20__ _____

20__ _____

July 23

"Writing in a journal activates the narrator function of our minds. Studies have suggested that simply writing down our account of a challenging experience can lower physiological reactivity and increase our sense of well-being, even if we never show what we've written to anyone else."
—Daniel J. Siegel[29]

20__ _____

20__ _____

20__ _____

20__ _____

20__ _____

---

29. https://quotefancy.com/quote/2500072/Daniel-J-Siegel-Writing-in-a-journal-activates-the-narrator-function-of-our-minds-Studies Accessed 28 January 2022.

July 24

How would it fit to acknowledge your basic emotions, today, here in your journal? Basic emotions include: happy, sad, mad, calm, afraid, worried, excited, hopeful, etc. Also, remember, it is perfectly fine and common to experience mixed emotions, too. For example, excitement about a new experience, mixed with some anxiety, topped off with hope that the opportunity works out well.

Simply finish the next sentence:
Today, when I consider repairing my life with gold, I feel:

20__ _____

20__ _____

20__ _____

20__ _____

20__ _____

Mrs. Valerie Christina Malicki, MA, LPCC, CPM

July 25
"Beautiful irony is when the very thing that destroyed you instead made you stronger."
—Anonymous

What is a powerful, good life lesson that you have, ironically, learned from a difficult, painful experience?

20__ _____

20__ _____

20__ _____

20__ _____

20__ _____

July 26

Through facing losses and various painful experiences, I learned that I had to choose to become bitter or to become better. I remember wanting to make my mom proud, versus allowing for excessive self-pity because of losing her physical presence. During milestone decision moments in life, I often pondered, what would my mom think about this? My mom would not want me to live a bitter, lonely life that resulted from some false beliefs of abandonment, or other unresolved emotional issues. Step by step, I began making the choice to become "better" rather than "bitter."

20__ _____

20__ _____

20__ _____

20__ _____

20__ _____

July 27

Considering your own trials, what is a step you may take toward "better," today? It could be reading a blog on emotional healing. It could be choosing to work with a professional in the area of your life that *most* yearns for repair. It could be choosing to journal at length about some painful feelings. It could be sharing openly with a friend who is truly supportive. It could be asking for God's wisdom for your next step toward choosing "better." What is a small, yet potentially life-changing step toward *repair* that you will *choose* to take in the next week?

20__ _____

20__ _____

20__ _____

20__ _____

20__ _____

July 28

Though my own journey has been painful at times, all the pressures have created unbreakable diamonds of Truth in my heart and soul. As I choose to be better, not bitter, I see the ways God blesses me, even in the midst of loss. Yes, some diamonds are *excruciating* diamonds to create—yet, somehow, they enable me to experience Truth, Goodness, and Grace. They make me keen to the fragility of life, the value of loving relationships, and the immense nature of legacy. I have lost my mother, sister, and a beloved grandmother in this life. Yet, I have gained three new little women—our three daughters. I have experienced family losses, yet I have also experienced the profound blessing of creating new, positive family times, experiences, and memories. For me, our sweet, fun family life has been the direct result of repair work, a priceless diamond deep in my heart.

20__ _____

20__ _____

20__ _____

20__ _____

20__ _____

July 29

"Every lie is a poison; there are no harmless lies. Only the truth gives me consolation—it is the one unbreakable diamond."
—Leo Tolstoy

20__ _____

20__ _____

20__ _____

20__ _____

20__ _____

July 30

"So take seriously the story that God has given you to live. It's time to read your own life, because your story is the one that could set us all ablaze."
—Dan B. Allender[30]

20__ _____

20__ _____

20__ _____

20__ _____

20__ _____

---

30. https://quotefancy.com/quote/1537118/Dan-B-Allender-So-take-seriously-the-story-that-God-has-given-you-to-live-It-s-time-to Accessed 5 February 2022.

Mrs. Valerie Christina Malicki, MA, LPCC, CPM

July 31

As we finish this chapter on repairing with gold, imagine receiving your broken pot, the one that is now repaired with gold. As you see with your own eyes the repairs, you are amazed! It is stunningly beautiful, with golden artwork that gorgeously repairs ALL the broken places. As you imagine your *repairing vision,* now, what are you hearing, tasting, smelling, seeing, and feeling?

I invite you to imagine fully *receiving* all the good things that this golden repair brings into your own beautifully transforming life.

20__ _____

20__ _____

20__ _____

20__ _____

20__ _____

At Eve's Joy Professional Mentoring
we specialize in pastoral care for women only.

We offer a unique, world-class blend of
faith-based, therapeutically-informed, certified
professional mentoring.

We would love to hear more about your unique *repairing vision*, and also provide you with specific next steps on how to continue to make it happen.

Simply drop us your current one-sentence *repairing vision* at EvesJoy.com. You can leave your confidential vision at the bottom of the home page where it says "Leave a message." With this simple entry, you apply to receive one of our periodic, free, confidential, exploration calls. An exploration call is guaranteed to be the best next step toward creating your own unique *repairing vision*.

Your completely confidential response helps us to create content that further supports you, such as: blogs, emails, webinars, summit/retreat topics, new online groups, podcasts, et cetera.

We are constantly creating new supportive content for you. Please drop us a line and let us know how we can support your next step toward becoming a woman of Wild Joy!

AUGUST

Become a Woman of Wild Joy Through *Daring*.

"It is not the critic who counts; not the man who points out how the strong man stumbles or where the doer of deeds could have done them better. The credit belongs to the man who is actually in the arena, whose face is marred by dust and sweat and blood; who strives valiantly; who errs, who comes short again and again, because there is no effort without error and shortcoming; but who does actually strive to do the deeds; who knows the great enthusiasms, the great devotions; who spends himself in a worthy cause; who at the best knows in the end the triumph of high achievement, and who at the worst, if he fails, at least fails while daring greatly, so that his place shall never be with those cold and timid souls who neither know victory nor defeat."
—Theodore Roosevelt[31]

Take 15 minutes to BE and ponder how you would dare to "be in the arena."

---

31. https://quotefancy.com/quote/1792613/Theodore-Roosevelt-It-is-not-the-critic-who-counts-not-the-one-who-points-out-how-the Accessed 11 December 2021.

What road before you requires courage? In what area of your life do you need to "take the bull by the horns" by acting with brave audacity? How will demonstrating daring and courage make your vision possible?

Do you need to end a toxic relationship? Do you need to quit a job that is not a good fit (for either party)? Do you need to finish a project you have been putting off? Maybe you've been putting off your own personal inner work of healing, or re-evaluating your priorities? In other words, is your actual big project a project of personal transformation?

In what way do you need to courageously "wake up and smell the coffee?"

Where do *you* need to have courage to focus on actually being in the arena?

Mrs. Valerie Christina Malicki, MA, LPCC, CPM

Where do you need to put a stake in the ground, have courage, and believe in your daring vision?

Simply write your answers below, for today, and then for each consecutive year.

This month, I dare to:

20__ _____

20__ _____

20__ _____

20__ _____

20__ _____

This is your daring vision for *today!*

In five years, I aspire to be *daring* in this way:

20__ _____

20__ _____

20__ _____

20__ _____

20__ _____

This is your long-term *daring vision for the future.*

Your vision today and your long-term vision connect, as one is like a stepping stone to the other. Both of these visions are a part of your own unique big picture of *daring*.

Your own unique big picture of *daring* is our focus for August.

·

This month, let's remember our mantra each day:

I become a woman of Wild Joy through *daring*.

Mrs. Valerie Christina Malicki, MA, LPCC, CPM

August 1

In my own journey, I needed courage to face the critics and keep going. Like a mentor suggested to me: "SMILE a knowing smile, and DO what you need to do." Basically, this means that I don't need to answer to those who are in the bleachers, criticizing, while I am in the arena "doing." This held true for me within the "arena" of homeschooling, for example.

(Ever notice when you have children, or do anything of significance in life, how some people *always* have a better way to do things—their way, of course? Yes, this can be a good time to SMILE, *and move on!*)

20__ _____

20__ _____

20__ _____

20__ _____

20__ _____

August 2

Sometimes, it actually is kind of fun to face critics with a smile. The fun is in knowing that no matter what, all the choices in my own life are made by me. It is my life, after all. What is the "arena" of your own daring vision?

20__ _____

20__ _____

20__ _____

20__ _____

20__ _____

Mrs. Valerie Christina Malicki, MA, LPCC, CPM

August 3
Have you ever experienced critics in the bleachers of your arena? How did you handle it? What did you learn?

20__ _____

20__ _____

20__ _____

20__ _____

20__ _____

August 4
"The greatest pleasure in life is
doing what people say you cannot do."
—Walter Bagehot

20__ _____

20__ _____

20__ _____

20__ _____

20__ _____

August 5
Ponder how "critics" may actually inspire you. Ponder the idea of, "Prove them wrong." What would it look like for you to prove your critics wrong?

20__ _____

20__ _____

20__ _____

20__ _____

20__ _____

August 6

"Whenever you're feeling controlled, demeaned, like they don't want you to do what you believe God has called you to do, that's a *big sign* that you're dealing with a toxic person."
—Gary Thomas[32]

20__ _____

20__ _____

20__ _____

20__ _____

20__ _____

---

[32] https://www.familylife.com/podcast/familylife-today/playing-spiritual-defense/ Accessed 7 August 2022.

August 7

Another "arena" for me has been
the arena of healthy relationships. At one point in
my journey, I realized I needed to have healthier
relationships by having healthier give and take. Healthier
boundaries and self-awareness of my own limits would help
me give and receive love in more mutual ways. For me,
sometimes, this takes a lot of courage and daring. Yet, the
work I did was, and continues to be, all worth it.
(My relationships are much better with mutual
give and take—obviously!)

20__ _____

20__ _____

20__ _____

20__ _____

20__ _____

August 8

In all the "arenas" in my life, I found that the more daring I displayed, the stronger I became. It must be like practicing mountain climbing regularly. I live in a very flat region, so I would not know about this from life experience. Yet, I imagine that in actual mountain climbing, with practice, the "rocky crags" and "steep climbs" must become easier and easier. I do find that when I show courage regularly, then, when it is most needed, I am in good practice. Every little daring act counts, and builds my "courage muscles."

20__ _____

20__ _____

20__ _____

20__ _____

20__ _____

Mrs. Valerie Christina Malicki, MA, LPCC, CPM

August 9

Maintaining healthy, positive, high-vibe relationships became one way I began to better "climb the mountain" of my own daring vision. What is one courageous way you could better "climb the mountain" of your own daring vision?

20__ _____

20__ _____

20__ _____

20__ _____

20__ _____

August 10
What movie, book, or story inspires you to be strong, energetic, courageous, determined, or brave? Why?

20__ _____

20__ _____

20__ _____

20__ _____

20__ _____

August 11

I love the hero in the movie *Schindler's List*. In the film—which is based on a true story—the hero used his influence positively. The hero saves hundreds of lives of Jews, even despite his own flaws. This story gives me courage to be daring, for the cause of good, despite my flaws. I invite you to ponder one courageous quality, or truth, found in one of your own favorite inspirational stories. What is one way you could apply this inspiring quality to your own vision of daring?

20__ _____

20__ _____

20__ _____

20__ _____

20__ _____

August 12

In another WW2 movie, *Hidden In Silence*, I get inspired by the young Catholic heroine's incredible perseverance and courage as she hid Jews, successfully, for months and months. This movie, based on a true story, ends with her lifelong marriage to one of the Jews she saved. She and her husband were able to live a free and good life with their family, after the war. I am immensely inspired as I ponder how her horrific story had a happy ending. Her daring made a difference in this world for good.

How will your *daring* make a difference in this world?

20__ _____

20__ _____

20__ _____

20__ _____

20__ _____

Mrs. Valerie Christina Malicki, MA, LPCC, CPM

August 13
If your life were an inspirational movie and you were the main character, what would this character be like?

20__ _____

20__ _____

20__ _____

20__ _____

20__ _____

August 14
Now, let's transform this into a video game, where the character that represents you is called an "avatar." How would your avatar be *daring*?

20__ _____

20__ _____

20__ _____

20__ _____

20__ _____

Mrs. Valerie Christina Malicki, MA, LPCC, CPM

August 15

Consider other details of the
"daring avatar" you chose for yourself. It's kind of a fun,
playful way to be brave and keep going in your own
"arenas." What are your avatar's
best superpowers?

20__ _____

20__ _____

20__ _____

20__ _____

20__ _____

August 16

One day I saw a meme of a homeschooling moms group being like a group of smart, successful, savvy, country-western outlaws. I lost it, because it was so hysterically true —especially about how talented and tough you have to be to actually survive and thrive!

20__ _____

20__ _____

20__ _____

20__ _____

20__ _____

Mrs. Valerie Christina Malicki, MA, LPCC, CPM

August 17
Reflecting on your own arena,
describe how the superpowers of
your daring avatar help her to dare, greatly.
What are her bold, new adventures?

20__ _____

20__ _____

20__ _____

20__ _____

20__ _____

August 18

What is your daring avatar's name? Nope,
I'm not kidding. For example, as a young child my daughter,
Rosie, enjoyed having an avatar of a superhero named
"Rosie Red."

20__ _____

20__ _____

20__ _____

20__ _____

20__ _____

August 19
"Do not dare not to dare."
—Aslan, C.S. Lewis,
The Horse and His Boy[33]

20__ _____

20__ _____

20__ _____

20__ _____

20__ _____

---

33. https://www.goodreads.com/quotes/56510-do-not-dare-not-to-dare Accessed 23 April 2022.

August 20

Spend time every day this month visualizing your own avatar. How would your own daring avatar handle *especially* difficult situations in *their* arena?

20__ _____

20__ _____

20__ _____

20__ _____

20__ _____

August 21
"Victory is always possible for
the person who refuses to stop fighting."
—Napoleon Hill

20__ _____

20__ _____

20__ _____

20__ _____

20__ _____

August 22

"Maybe everything comes out all right, if you keep on trying. Anyway, you have to keep on trying; nothing will come out right if you don't."
—Laura Ingalls Wilder,
These Happy Golden Years [34]

20__ _____

20__ _____

20__ _____

20__ _____

20__ _____

---

[34] https://www.goodreads.com/work/quotes/4132-these-happy-golden-years Accessed 14 February 2022.

Mrs. Valerie Christina Malicki, MA, LPCC, CPM

August 23
"Do just once what others say you can't do, and you will never pay attention to their limitations again."
—James Cook

20__ _____

20__ _____

20__ _____

20__ _____

20__ _____

August 24

"Courage means to follow the heart. There are millions of women who commit acts of great heart every day. It is not only the singular act that reshapes a dry collective, but also the continuation of those acts. As a young Buddist nun once told me, 'Water drips through stone.'"
—Clarissa Pinkola Estes,
Women Who Run With Wolves[35]

20__ _____

20__ _____

20__ _____

20__ _____

20__ _____

---

35. Clarissa Pinkola Estés, Ph.D., ***Women Who Run With Wolves*** (New York: Ballantine Books, 1992).

Mrs. Valerie Christina Malicki, MA, LPCC, CPM

August 25

After the birth of my second child, I discovered a horrifically toxic industrial wind turbine project was scheduled to be built 765 feet from our family home. The more I learned about the impact to those living nearby (like my kids), the more I couldn't believe these toxic projects were even allowed to be built near homes. Residents around the globe experience a lower standard of living in *lucky* cases, and headaches, insomnia, and a host of health *and* life problems in many, more severe cases. I personally met wind turbine victims and learned of their tragic, real-life stories. The entire project seemed to be a huge, stone Goliath. Yet, over seven *years,* our very small community—with the immense support of other warriors around the world—put a stop to this project. I saw firsthand that water really does drip *through* stone.

20__ _____

20__ _____

20__ _____

20__ _____

20__ _____

August 26

"Rise like Lions after slumber
In unvanquishable number—
Shake your chains to earth like dew
Which in sleep had fallen on you
Ye are many—they are few."
—Percy Bysshe Shelley,
The Masque of Anarchy[36]

20__ _____

20__ _____

20__ _____

20__ _____

20__ _____

---

36. https://poets.org/poem/mask-anarchy-excerpt Accessed 14 February 2022.

August 27
"Until the lion learns how to write, every story will glorify the hunter."
—J. Nozipo Maraire

20__ _____

20__ _____

20__ _____

20__ _____

20__ _____

August 28

"Be prepared that the people closest to you in your life may not be able to recognize the profound nature of what you have to offer this world. Follow your heart—live into your dreams for yourself, even if those in your family or hometown cannot recognize the greatness within you. Ground yourself in the light that burns within—and follow it,"
(from personal correspondence on Dec. 7, 2020).
—Rev. Dr. Darcy Metcalfe, Assistant Professor of Religious Studies, University of Findlay

20__ _____

20__ _____

20__ _____

20__ _____

20__ _____

Mrs. Valerie Christina Malicki, MA, LPCC, CPM

August 29
"Sometimes the people around you won't understand your journey. They don't need to, it's not for them."
—Joubert Botha

20__ _____

20__ _____

20__ _____

20__ _____

20__ _____

August 30

"The woman who does not require validation from anyone, is the most feared individual on the planet."
—Mohadesa Najumi

20__ _____

20__ _____

20__ _____

20__ _____

20__ _____

August 31

Imagine your avatar developing a *daring* mantra. It could be something like, "No one is me, and that is my superpower," or, "When odds are one in a million, be that one!" What mantra would *your* avatar develop about all the *daring* lessons learned this month?

20__ _____

20__ _____

20__ _____

20__ _____

20__ _____

At Eve's Joy Professional Mentoring
we specialize in pastoral care for women only.

We offer a unique, world-class blend of
faith-based, therapeutically-informed, certified
professional mentoring.

We would love to hear more about your
unique *daring vision*, and also provide you with specific
next steps on how to continue to
make it happen.

Simply drop us your current one-sentence
daring vision at EvesJoy.com. You can leave your
confidential vision at the bottom of the home page where it
says "Leave a message." With this simple entry, you apply
to receive one of our periodic, free, confidential, exploration
calls. An exploration call is guaranteed to be the best next
step toward creating your own
unique *daring vision*.

Your completely confidential response helps
us to create content that further supports you, such as:
blogs, emails, webinars, summit/retreat topics, new online
groups, podcasts, et cetera.

We are constantly creating new supportive
content for you. Please drop us a line, and let us know how
we can support your next step toward becoming a woman
of Wild Joy!

SEPTEMBER

Become a Woman of Wild Joy Through *Rising*.

"You may write me down in history
With your bitter, twisted lies,
You may trod me in the very dirt
But still, like dust, I'll rise.
(...)
Out of the huts of history's shame
I rise
Up from a past that's rooted in pain
I rise
I'm a black ocean, leaping and wide,
Welling and swelling I bear in the tide.
Leaving behind nights of terror and fear
I rise
Into a daybreak that's wondrously clear
I rise
Bringing the gifts that my ancestors gave,
I am the dream and the hope of the slave.
I rise
I rise
I rise."
-Maya Angelou[37]

What is one area or circumstance where you have felt shame, fear, pain, or even terror?

---

37. https://www.poetryfoundation.org/poems/46446/still-i-rise Accessed 12 February 2022.

This month, let's reflect on an area of life where you have felt defeated. Imagine, the best you are able to right now, the transformation of your difficult, negative, setback area. Imagine this area becoming a springboard to a thriving, positive comeback. We will expand on this positive comeback vision together this month.

Take 15 minutes, undisturbed and focused. This month, we will expand your vision of *rising*. Joy happens, more and more, as we rise in areas of life that matter to us. You may yearn to rise in love, in confidence, in prosperity, in experiencing a peaceful home life, in work, in self-care, in healthy boundaries, in healthy relationships, in true intimacy, in friendship, in competence, or in whatever area comes to your heart. You may yearn to rise in creativity, in your spiritual growth, in your purpose, or in delighting in "the ordinary" right before your eyes.

Mrs. Valerie Christina Malicki, MA, LPCC, CPM

In what area of your life
do you most want to *rise* this month?

Simply finish this sentence,
today, and then each consecutive year:

This month, *I will rise* in this way:

20__ _____

20__ _____

20__ _____

20__ _____

20__ _____

This is *your* focus and unique rising vision.

This month, we remember our mantra, below:

**I become a woman of Wild Joy
through *rising*.**

September 1

Imagine yourself *rising* in the area of your choice. Fully experience, in your imagination, this *rising vision.* For example, if you want to rise in romance, imagine *actually* experiencing your heart's desire in this area. When I, myself, wanted to experience romance, I imagined experiencing the smell of roses, the sound of a sweet compliment, the taste of chocolates (or, one of my favorites, flavored coffee), the feel of a warm hug, and the sight of my love smiling at me. I envisioned smiling as he invited me on a hot date. I even imagined snuggling and talking, undistracted, at home together. All this, and more, has happened in real life for me. A *rising vision* can be powerful. Yes, imagining is a *powerful* form of planning!

Let's return to your own unique vision of rising. As you imagine powerfully rising in this area, what are you seeing, tasting, smelling, hearing, and feeling?

20__ _____

20__ _____

20__ _____

20__ _____

20__ _____

Mrs. Valerie Christina Malicki, MA, LPCC, CPM

September 2

When I desired to rise in romance.
I began to explore what was romantic *for me*. I began to add more and more and more details that were definitely part of my heart's desire. Hearing sweet talk was a part of my expanded vision of rising in romance. In every area we want to rise, there are details that are unique for our own circumstances and lives.

20__ _____

20__ _____

20__ _____

20__ _____

20__ _____

September 3

"You are the finest, loveliest, tenderest,
and most beautiful person I have ever known and even that
is an understatement."
—F. Scott Fitzgerald

20__ _____

20__ _____

20__ _____

20__ _____

20__ _____

Mrs. Valerie Christina Malicki, MA, LPCC, CPM

September 4

I wanted to rise in the area of romance after feeling the spark and passion in my relationship fade. I knew we needed change for our relationship to survive and thrive through each life change, such as birthing a new child. We both began to first acknowledge that we wanted something different, something better. The awareness that we wanted change was a first step. Having children was more stressful than we both imagined! One way we began turning our relationship back around was in making time for just us—guilt-free. If that meant another video for the kids while we had time alone, so be it. We limit screen-time in our home anyway, to accommodate those times. It was essential for us to give our marriage the time and energy we both needed. This nourishing "water" to the soil of our relationship helped make those romantic feelings flourish again. It has been said: "The grass is greenest where you water it!"

20__ _____

20__ _____

20__ _____

20__ _____

20__ _____

September 5

Thankfully, by nourishing our relationship, we were able to turn this romance setback into a romance comeback. As we watered the soil of our connection, the green grass grew and grew and grew. These days, we have lots of sweet connection times that help make our marriage thrive. Also, we share tasks and plan for individual times, too, that make our marriage feel compatible and comfortable. This is just one of many areas in my life where a setback has become a springboard to a comeback.

In the past, in any area of your life, have you ever turned a setback into a comeback? If not, in what way do you wish you had experienced a comeback?

20__ _____

20__ _____

20__ _____

20__ _____

20__ _____

Mrs. Valerie Christina Malicki, MA, LPCC, CPM

September 6
"It is impossible for you to go as you were before, so you must go on as you never have."
—Cheryl Strayed

20__ _____

20__ _____

20__ _____

20__ _____

20__ _____

September 7

At times, when we yearn to rise, we must learn an entirely new set of habits. If we yearn for A, then we must learn to do B habitually. For example, when I wanted to rise as a home educator, I began focusing on teaching reading. I wanted my children to learn to read well, "A." So, I began a small habit of spending 20 minutes every day reading together, "B."

What new habit would support your vision? Do you need to develop the "B" habit of drinking more water, exercising regularly, spending time building healthy friendships, or saving money, to achieve your true "A" plan? What is one new habit that will bring you closer to your unique vision of rising?

20__ _____

20__ _____

20__ _____

20__ _____

20__ _____

Mrs. Valerie Christina Malicki, MA, LPCC, CPM

September 8

So many of my comebacks have come from setbacks. These days, I am in my self-care comeback season. A new habit that helps me stay in this season is my daily 15-minute morning prayer time. Though it may seem small, it was one foundational step that really helped me to rise above in the area of self-care. What is one, new, daily 15-minute habit that would support your rising vision?

20__ _____

20__ _____

20__ _____

20__ _____

20__ _____

September 9

It has been said it takes 21 days to form a habit. How would it fit to begin practicing one, *new*, daily foundational habit that will support you in your vision of rising? How would it fit to implement this new, daily, 15-minute habit every day for the rest of the month?

20__ _____

20__ _____

20__ _____

20__ _____

20__ _____

September 10

"I am always doing what I cannot do yet, in order to learn how to do it."
—Vincent Van Gogh

20__ _____

20__ _____

20__ _____

20__ _____

20__ _____

September 11

Imagine looking back on your life at this time next year and feeling sad because you did not rise. Imagine you settled by accepting mediocre instead of striving for amazing. In the area that you want to experience rising, what does it look like to *not* rise? Let this yucky feeling of mediocrity motivate you. Let's focus on rising to the level of "amazing" by putting a stake in the ground, today.

Repeat after me: Today, I *choose* to *rise* above.

20__ _____

20__ _____

20__ _____

20__ _____

20__ _____

Mrs. Valerie Christina Malicki, MA, LPCC, CPM

September 12

What actions brought you to the circumstances you now want to change? Let's press pause—and also press reset—with this situation. What is one negative action in your life that does not contribute to your rising vision? Maybe it is the self-sabotage of procrastination, an addiction, a toxic relationship style, or recurring negative thinking, for example. How will you work toward eliminating this one negative action today?

20__ _____

20__ _____

20__ _____

20__ _____

20__ _____

September 13
"Sometimes the harder you fall,
the stronger you rise."
—Anonymous

20__ _____

20__ _____

20__ _____

20__ _____

20__ _____

September 14

"The definition of insanity is doing the same thing over and over, but expecting different results."
—Anonymous

20__ _____

20__ _____

20__ _____

20__ _____

20__ _____

September 15

"Believe in yourself, still. Sometimes the last mistake and regret leads to the next miracle and reawakening."
—Brendon Burchard

20__ _____

20__ _____

20__ _____

20__ _____

20__ _____

Mrs. Valerie Christina Malicki, MA, LPCC, CPM

September 16

As you consider your own unique vision of rising, ponder a few more details that will expand your vision. For example, at one time, I wanted to have more authentic, mutual connection in my relationships. I also wanted my relationships to be more mutually positive and supportive. What are some further details that expand your own unique vision of rising?

20__ _____

20__ _____

20__ _____

20__ _____

20__ _____

September 17

Now that you have expanded your unique vision of rising, imagine actually experiencing it. You are climbing to the very top of your mountain, and now, *voila*, you have reached the top! How does your vision of rising sound, feel, taste, smell, and look, now?

20__ _____

20__ _____

20__ _____

20__ _____

20__ _____

Mrs. Valerie Christina Malicki, MA, LPCC, CPM

September 18
"You don't have to move mountains. Simply fall in love with life. Be a tornado of happiness, gratitude, and acceptance. You will change the world by just being a warm, kind-hearted human being."
—Anita Krizzan[38]

20__ _____

20__ _____

20__ _____

20__ _____

20__ _____

---

38. https://www.dictionary-quotes.com/anita-krizzan/ Accessed 12 February 2022.

September 19

At one point, I wanted to rise in the area of impact. I imagined being more and more blessed as a family so that, as a family, we were able to bless others more and more. We often consider blessing others with money, yet, often simple kindnesses make more of an impact than we realize.

20__ _____

20__ _____

20__ _____

20__ _____

20__ _____

September 20

"Kindness is the greatest wealth of all.
Small acts of kindness last longer than a lifetime. This lesson, that kindness and generosity and faith in your fellow man are more important than money, is the first and greatest lesson my father ever taught me. And in this way he will always be with us and always
live forever."
—Eddie Jaku,
The Happiest Man on Earth[39]

20__ _____

20__ _____

20__ _____

20__ _____

20__ _____

---

39. Eddie Jaku, ***The Happiest Man On Earth: The Beautiful Life of an Auschwitz Survivor***, (New York, NY: Harper an Imprint of HarperCollins Publishers, 2021).

September 21

As I pondered our family's impact, one way I wanted to grow was in the area of making others feel welcomed and appreciated and valued. I also knew I needed to lead by example.

20__ _____

20__ _____

20__ _____

20__ _____

20__ _____

Mrs. Valerie Christina Malicki, MA, LPCC, CPM

September 22
"All the other dogs do whatever the lead dog does. So the lead dog has to be the smartest and strongest dog of all."
—Natalie Standiford,
The Bravest Dog Ever: The Story of Balto[40]

20__ _____

20__ _____

20__ _____

20__ _____

20__ _____

---
40. Natalie Standiford, ***The Bravest Dog Ever: The Story of Balto***, (New York: Random House, 1989).

September 23
How will your rising vision allow you,
and require you, to be *smart and strong*, and to
lead by example?

20__ _____

20__ _____

20__ _____

20__ _____

20__ _____

Mrs. Valerie Christina Malicki, MA, LPCC, CPM

September 24

Let's ponder being a good example with your intelligence. It has been said there are at least a dozen forms of intelligence, such as mechanical, musical, interpersonal, and mathematical. What is one area of your life where *you* show competence and ability?

(Everyone has gifts. I invite you to ask for input from trustworthy friends if you need help seeing your gifts.)

20__ _____

20__ _____

20__ _____

20__ _____

20__ _____

September 25

Imagine combining your past strengths and your past intelligences. Then, you may use these abilities in your rising vision. For example, in grade school I wanted to work hard on my long jump. Our class was working on a physical fitness test, and this was one of the tests. I learned and practiced long jump techniques with a library book. (My dad advised me to do this. My mother brought us to the local library often.) I ended up winning a rather prestigious physical fitness award as a result of my efforts. That may seem silly now, or irrelevant. Yet, today I can still tap into those learned qualities of resourcefulness, perseverance, and healthy living.

How will you combine your strengths and smarts to contribute to your rising vision?

20__ _____

20__ _____

20__ _____

20__ _____

20__ _____

Mrs. Valerie Christina Malicki, MA, LPCC, CPM

September 26

As we expand your own unique vision of rising, what would it taste, feel, sound, smell, and look like if you expanded your vision by one hundred?

Summarize your expanded rising vision below. Next year, check in with how you are doing.

One time I did this, and here's what I had to say: "You've come a long way, baby!"

It will be exciting to see your own unique growth, year after year. Whoohoo!

20__ _____

20__ _____

20__ _____

20__ _____

20__ _____

September 27

Imagine that a world-class mentor, whose life you admired, is having an individual session with you today. What would they say to emphatically support, guide, and inspire you? How would they cheer you on in your own unique *rising vision?*
Write it here:

20__ _____

20__ _____

20__ _____

20__ _____

20__ _____

Mrs. Valerie Christina Malicki, MA, LPCC, CPM

September 28
Repeat after me: With God's Grace,
I *am* unstoppable in my rising!

20__ _____

20__ _____

20__ _____

20__ _____

20__ _____

September 29

"...for though the righteous
fall seven times, they rise again..."
—Proverbs 24:16a, NIV

How are you doing with practicing that one,
new, daily, 15-minute habit that you chose 21 days ago?
I invite you to keep going. And when you
fall, choose to rise again!

20__ _____

20__ _____

20__ _____

20__ _____

20__ _____

Mrs. Valerie Christina Malicki, MA, LPCC, CPM

September 30
As we are coming to a close in this area of rising, what is the biggest lesson you, personally, are learning about your own unique vision of rising?

20__ _____

20__ _____

20__ _____

20__ _____

20__ _____

At Eve's Joy Professional Mentoring
we specialize in pastoral care for women only.

We offer a unique, world-class blend of
faith-based, therapeutically-informed, certified
professional mentoring.

We would love to hear more about your unique *rising vision*, and also provide you with specific next steps on how to continue to make it happen.

Simply drop us your current one-sentence *rising vision* at EvesJoy.com. You can leave your confidential vision at the bottom of the home page where it says "Leave a message." With this simple entry, you apply to receive one of our periodic, free, confidential, exploration calls. An exploration call is guaranteed to be the best next step toward creating your own
unique *rising vision*.

Your completely confidential response helps
us to create content that further supports you, such as:
blogs, emails, webinars, summit/retreat topics, new online
groups, podcasts, et cetera.

We are constantly creating new supportive
content for you. Please drop us a line, and let us know how
we can support your next step toward becoming a
woman of Wild Joy!

OCTOBER

Become a Woman of Wild Joy Through *Soaring*.

"No bird soars too high…with his own wings."
—William Blake

Take 15 minutes to fully imagine an aspect of your life in which you most yearn to really soar, really come alive, really rise *above*, and really *stay* above for good. The way you yearn to *soar* may be in work, in actually following through with good self-care once and for all, or in finally eliminating that toxic situation from your life. Ponder what area is most calling to you.

How would it be to experience *soaring* in work, play, love, or in any area of life that you choose?

Becoming a Woman of Wild Joy

We will expand this *soaring vision* together this month. For now, simply finish the next sentence, today and each consecutive year:

Today, my *soaring vision* looks like this:

20__ _____

20__ _____

20__ _____

20__ _____

20__ _____

This is your unique *soaring vision* and focus for October. Every day, remember our mantra for this month:

I become a woman of Wild Joy through *soaring*.

Mrs. Valerie Christina Malicki, MA, LPCC, CPM

October 1

Imagine one area of your life where you will begin to really *soar* this month. Fully imagine this experience of *soaring*. For example, imagine soaring in the area of confidence. Soaring in the area of confidence may be, for one thing, like happily feeling God's Love for who you truly are in the depths of your being. How do *you* yearn to soar? I invite you to mentally focus and imagine your own unique *soaring vision*. Today, as you imagine your *soaring vision*, what do you hear, smell, feel, taste, and see?

20__ _____

20__ _____

20__ _____

20__ _____

20__ _____

October 2

As I begin my lift-off into times of soaring, music often keeps me going strong. I find empowering, uplifting music and listen to it (sometimes a bit obsessively) on repeat. It lifts my mood, my emotions, and my thoughts into a positive, high-vibing realm. This high-vibe realm is crucial to my soaring success.

What song describes your soaring focus this month? This song may also be the "music" of morning birds chirping, for example. This "music" may be the quiet peacefulness of silence. Simply choose music that truly, undeniably, lifts your spirits and makes you smile. Choose music that gives you energy and refreshes your heart. I invite you to *listen* to this music and imagine yourself fully experiencing your *soaring vision*.

20__ _____

20__ _____

20__ _____

20__ _____

20__ _____

Mrs. Valerie Christina Malicki, MA, LPCC, CPM

October 3

As I began my own experience of soaring as a wife and mom, I had to totally tune out circumstances around me. The tune I had to listen for above the noise was the "music" I was authentically creating in my own life.

20__ _____

20__ _____

20__ _____

20__ _____

20__ _____

October 4
I developed my own mantra: She who leads the orchestra must turn her back to the crowd!

20__ _____

20__ _____

20__ _____

20__ _____

20__ _____

Mrs. Valerie Christina Malicki, MA, LPCC, CPM

October 5
As I turn my back to the crowd and create "music" in life, I remember:

With God's help, I am a powerful co-creator!

20__ _____

20__ _____

20__ _____

20__ _____

20__ _____

October 6

"The cave you fear to enter holds the treasure you seek."
—Joseph Campbell

20__

20__

20__

20__

20__

October 7

On my journey, I often choose to enter caves that I fear. Yes, it is hard. Yet, inevitably, there are rich treasures in store. Many times, there are a myriad of facets—and fears—to my own Joy-seeking story. Sometimes it is hard to see God's gracious Providence. Sometimes I don't want to face my buried anger, or my struggles in believing in God's Goodness, or even my yearning to magnificently *soar*. Yet, I do yearn to experience *soaring* in my work, my play, my love, and my whole life.

What is a cave you fear?

20__ _____

20__ _____

20__ _____

20__ _____

20__ _____

October 8

If I'm honest, at times, I fear perhaps God
is holding out on me—especially when it comes to my
work. Well, and my relationships. And, also my play. OK,
sometimes it is hard to trust at all, and sometimes it is
especially hard to trust in God. I'm not a fearful person by
nature, but there are certain caves I did successfully
avoid for a time. Yet, I need to face these fears
—especially about God—
in order to have the
treasures I seek.

20__ _____

20__ _____

20__ _____

20__ _____

20__ _____

October 9

"...God is the storyteller
and Providence is his own storyline."
—Patti Callahan,
Becoming Mrs. Lewis[41]

20__ _____

20__ _____

20__ _____

20__ _____

20__ _____

---

41. Patti Callahan Henry, **Becoming Mrs. Lewis** (Nashville, TN: Thomas Nelson, registered trademark of HarperCollins Christian Publishing, Inc., 2018).

October 10

"It is as impossible for man to demonstrate the existence of God as it would be for even Sherlock Holmes to demonstrate the existence of Arthur Conan Doyle."
—Frederick Buechner[42]

20__ _____

20__ _____

20__ _____

20__ _____

20__ _____

---

42. https://www.frederickbuechner.com/quote-of-the-day/2017/10/6/god Accessed 6 February 2022.

October 11
"There is nothing more deceptive than an obvious fact."
—Arthur Conan Doyle

20__ _____

20__ _____

20__ _____

20__ _____

20__ _____

October 12

"I had always felt life first as a story: and if there is a story, there is a story-teller."
—G.K. Chesterton

20__ _____

20__ _____

20__ _____

20__ _____

20__ _____

Mrs. Valerie Christina Malicki, MA, LPCC, CPM

October 13

Through prayer, circumstances, and many blessed experiences, I continue to come into more and more understanding about God's Goodness. Through the ups, downs, and arounds, I am trusting in His good plans for me. Yes, He has good plans for me. Even many of the hard times in my life, I can now see, have prepared me and expanded me to live my Destiny. When I pause to reflect, I can see that God's Providential Goodness is interwoven throughout my entire life. All this is really too amazing to even comprehend.

As you pause to reflect, in what ways can you see Providential Goodness in your own life?

20__ _____

20__ _____

20__ _____

20__ _____

20__ _____

October 14

I realize that another cave I fear is that of not being "enough." I fear I am not able to do the hard work of learning to really soar. Sometimes, just saying we "can't" is easier than working on how we *can*. I realize I fear not being enough in many ways. For example, I fear I will never really be able to be thoroughly loving and patient with my kids. What about the constant challenge of their "day in and day out" needs, issues, questions, messes, meals, and mounds of laundry?

How is your *soaring vision* calling you to be the fullest and highest version of yourself?

20__ _____

20__ _____

20__ _____

20__ _____

20__ _____

Mrs. Valerie Christina Malicki, MA, LPCC, CPM

October 15
Repeat after me: I *can* do hard things!

20__ _____

20__ _____

20__ _____

20__ _____

20__ _____

October 16

I also yearn to practice *soaring* in all my various relationships. Knowing that I can do hard things, I bravely speak the truth in my relationships. I choose to assertively communicate regarding thoughts, feelings, needs, and mutual, healthy support. It feels so good to *practice, in real life,* relationship skills I have *learned for years.*

What is one way that you can *practice* what you have *learned*, so that you may soar?

20__ _____

20__ _____

20__ _____

20__ _____

20__ _____

Mrs. Valerie Christina Malicki, MA, LPCC, CPM

October 17
"If you would hit the mark, you must aim a little above it. Every arrow that flies feels the attraction of earth."
—Henry Wadsworth Longfellow

20___ _____

20___ _____

20___ _____

20___ _____

20___ _____

October 18
"The most effective way to do it, is to do it."
—Amelia Earhart

20__ _____

20__ _____

20__ _____

20__ _____

20__ _____

Mrs. Valerie Christina Malicki, MA, LPCC, CPM

October 19

In order to soar more and more, I needed to become what I like to call a "goal crusher." If I press "pause" too long on my tasks, they just explode. Like dishes that are not washed, they do not just go away. Yikes! At first, it may feel a little dramatic to think about "crushing" goals. Yet, I have found that truly crushing goals is an essential aspect of experiencing the satisfaction of *soaring*.

20__ _____

20__ _____

20__ _____

20__ _____

20__ _____

October 20
"You have to be odd to be number one."
—Dr. Seuss

20__

20__

20__

20__

20__

Mrs. Valerie Christina Malicki, MA, LPCC, CPM

October 21

I accomplish soaring, and crushing goals, by reaching for SMART goals. SMART goals are goals that are: Specific, Measurable, Attainable, Realistic, and Timely. I often prioritize three goals in the morning that are on my "must do" goal list.

My goals may be about: writing work, business errands, specific homeschool lessons (like a second grade arithmetic lesson), laundry (again!), my self-care practices (like taking a long country walk), etc. The list of my possible goals is basically endless, because I juggle so many things, daily.

What SMART goal will help you become a goal crusher and *do* the work of soaring, today?

20__ _____

20__ _____

20__ _____

20__ _____

20__ _____

October 22

"I think women are foolish to pretend
they are equal to men. They are far superior and always
have been. Whatever you give a woman,
she will make greater."
—William Golding

What, in your life, would you like to be "greater?"

20__ _____

20__ _____

20__ _____

20__ _____

20__ _____

Mrs. Valerie Christina Malicki, MA, LPCC, CPM

October 23

I also set—and aim to *achieve*—weekly, monthly, and yearly goals. One year I wanted to focus on my eldest daughter's reading—all year. These days, she is reading like a champ; I can't stop her from ordering new books to borrow from our library. Other years I have set goals like, "It is time to declutter!" Yearly, monthly, and weekly goals are all a part of *soaring*.

What SMART goal, for the next week, month, or year, will help you *do* the work of soaring, and therefore experience more Wild Joy?

20__ _____

20__ _____

20__ _____

20__ _____

20__ _____

October 24

"Don't live the same year 75 times and call it a life."
—Robin Sharma

20__ _____

20__ _____

20__ _____

20__ _____

20__ _____

Mrs. Valerie Christina Malicki, MA, LPCC, CPM

October 25
"You satisfy my every desire with good things. You've supercharged my life so that I soar again like a flying eagle in the sky!"
—Psalms 103:5, TPT

20__ _____

20__ _____

20__ _____

20__ _____

20__ _____

October 26

Yes, the more I achieved these SMART goals, the more I experienced *soaring*. Some days, it means making a list that is checked off. Other days, it means achieving a "goal" of resting, relaxing, and only doing light work. This would mean my goal for the day is to have a "mental health day." All of these various goals "count." SMART goals help me *do it*, meaning, they help me achieve my goal, become a goal crusher, and therefore, truly *soar*.

20__ _____

20__ _____

20__ _____

20__ _____

20__ _____

Mrs. Valerie Christina Malicki, MA, LPCC, CPM

October 27

How might you multiply and enlarge your own vision of soaring? Pause, ponder, and imagine your soaring vision expanded by one hundred. With your expanded vision, imagine soaring, now, in the area of your choice. What are you hearing, tasting, smelling, seeing, and feeling, now?

20__ _____

20__ _____

20__ _____

20__ _____

20__ _____

October 28
"I am ready, ready, ready
to elevate my mind to the high calling of Destiny."
—T.D. Jakes[43]

20__ _____

20__ _____

20__ _____

20__ _____

20__ _____

---

43. T.D.Jakes, ***Destiny Journal: Recording Your Path to a Life of Divine Order*** (New York, New York: Faith Words, Hachette Book Group, 2016 by TDJ Enterprises, LLP).

October 29

"One can never consent to creep when one feels an impulse to soar."
—Helen Keller

20__ _____

20__ _____

20__ _____

20__ _____

20__ _____

October 30

"How far I've come! I'm the same girl and yet not the same. I wonder if it's always like that? Folks keep growing from one person into another all their lives, and life is just a lot of everyday adventures. Well, whatever life is, I like it."
—Carol Ryrie Brink, ***Caddie Woodlawn***[44]

20__ _____

20__ _____

20__ _____

20__ _____

20__ _____

---

44. Carol Ryrie Brink, ***Caddie Woodlawn*** (New York, NY: Aladdin Paperbacks, An imprint of Simon &Schuster Children's Publishing Division, First Aladdin Paperbacks Edition, 1990).

Mrs. Valerie Christina Malicki, MA, LPCC, CPM

October 31

We are coming to a close in our month of focusing on your *soaring vision.* Ponder having your own feeling of, "How far I've come!"

What kind of person do you yearn to continue to "grow into" as you experience everyday adventures and *soar?*

20__ _____

20__ _____

20__ _____

20__ _____

20__ _____

At Eve's Joy Professional Mentoring
we specialize in pastoral care for women only.

We offer a unique, world-class blend of
faith-based, therapeutically-informed, certified
professional mentoring.

We would love to hear more about your unique *soaring vision*, and also provide you with specific next steps on how to continue to make it happen.

Simply drop us your current one-sentence
soaring vision at EvesJoy.com. You can leave your confidential vision at the bottom of the home page where it says "Leave a message." With this simple entry, you apply to receive one of our periodic, free, confidential, exploration calls. An exploration call is guaranteed to be the best next step toward creating your own
unique *soaring vision*.

Your completely confidential response helps
us to create content that further supports you, such as: blogs, emails, webinars, summit/retreat topics, new online groups, podcasts, et cetera.

We are constantly creating new supportive
content for you. Please drop us a line, and let us know how we can support your next step toward becoming
a woman of Wild Joy!

NOVEMBER

Become a Woman of Wild Joy
Through *Nesting*.

"Canceling plans is OK. Staying home is OK. Disappearing for a bit to get your life together is OK...It's called self-care."
—Kevin Farzad

One way to easily describe nesting is:
disappearing for a bit to get your life together!

Nesting is an outward experience of creating lovely environments, and it is an inward experience of creating lovely environments within, i.e., with a healthy mind and spirit. Nesting is a holistic experience of coming home to oneself in a place that is inviting, comfortable, and, well, "homey."

Solitude is being alone, even if only in mind and spirit. (You can "disappear" in a crowded room, and return "home" on the inside.) Yet, solitude is knowing that you are not alone. Solitude is knowing that you are with yourself, and that the God of The Universe is also with you.

Take 15 minutes and imagine your own ideal nesting experience this month. When do you especially yearn to be and feel at home—within, and also externally? Do you want to have a regular time to experience rest in your physical home? Do you yearn for inner peace during a "noisy" part of your life? As you ponder "coming home," what do you see, hear, taste, smell, and feel?

How do you yearn to experience an outward and inward space of comfort, rejuvenation, peacefulness, and being "at home"?

Mrs. Valerie Christina Malicki, MA, LPCC, CPM

Simply complete this sentence, this year, and each consecutive year:

I yearn to experience *nesting* in this way:

20__ _____

20__ _____

20__ _____

20__ _____

20__ _____

This is our *nesting vision* and focus for November. Every day, remember our mantra for the month:

I become a woman of Wild Joy through *nesting*.

November 1

What would it be like to create a world within, where you are "at home," just as you are, just being yourself? Would your life experience change, or would it stay the same?

20__ _____

20__ _____

20__ _____

20__ _____

20__ _____

November 2

"Solitude well practiced will break the power of busyness, haste, isolation, and loneliness."
—Dallas Willard

20__ _____

20__ _____

20__ _____

20__ _____

20__ _____

November 3

"I am now quite cured of seeking pleasure in society, be it country or town. A sensible man ought to find sufficient company in himself."
—Emily Bronte,
Wuthering Heights[45]

20__ _____

20__ _____

20__ _____

20__ _____

20__ _____

---

45. https://quotes.thefamouspeople.com/emily-bront-1342.php Accessed 11 December 2021.

Mrs. Valerie Christina Malicki, MA, LPCC, CPM

November 4
What would it be like, for you, to be happy with your own company?

20__ _____

20__ _____

20__ _____

20__ _____

20__ _____

November 5

"Now and then it's good to pause in
our pursuit of happiness and just be happy."
—Guillaume Apollinaire

20__ _____

20__ _____

20__ _____

20__ _____

20__ _____

Mrs. Valerie Christina Malicki, MA, LPCC, CPM

November 6

"Your kitchen is full. You make yourself nutritious meals. You don't need...toxic sustenance and try to make cookies out of crumbs."
—Melanie Tonia Evans

20__ _____

20__ _____

20__ _____

20__ _____

20__ _____

November 7
"No more crumbs."
—Alan Robarge

20__ _____

20__ _____

20__ _____

20__ _____

20__ _____

Mrs. Valerie Christina Malicki, MA, LPCC, CPM

November 8

It felt good to let go of chasing situations or people or even dreams that were, essentially, begging for crumbs. I make my own nutritious meals now. My soul is feasting on the inside. I am home within myself, and continually making an actual, outward home life, where we are happy.

20__ _____

20__ _____

20__ _____

20__ _____

20__ _____

November 9

"Happiness, not in another place but this place...not for another hour, but this hour."
—Walt Whitman

20__ _____

20__ _____

20__ _____

20__ _____

20__ _____

Mrs. Valerie Christina Malicki, MA, LPCC, CPM

November 10

I deeply savor Joy-Filled moments when
I take and make time away from posting and enjoy life to
the fullest. No "liking"—just living,
laughing, and loving—for real.

I invite you to enjoy some unplugged time
as you see, savor, taste, smell, hear, and feel goodness
and beauty in the world around you. I invite you to discover
or rediscover the joy of a life unplugged. I invite you to
"come home" to yourself, and to find
happiness from within.

How would it fit to check your mindset,
heart, and soul more often than you do your social media,
email, and phone?

20__ _____

20__ _____

20__ _____

20__ _____

20__ _____

November 11

How will you savor life, unplugged, each day? What times will you unplug daily to savor the world around you? I invite you to make and take time away from it all. I invite you to set aside time where you choose, for yourself, to be free of posting, liking, emailing, and screens—just living, laughing, and loving.

Pictures can be worth 1000 words, yet, looking into the eyes of the ones you love, deeply savoring the beautiful world all around...this is indescribably precious. How will you live, laugh, and love, today?

20__ _____

20__ _____

20__ _____

20__ _____

20__ _____

Mrs. Valerie Christina Malicki, MA, LPCC, CPM

November 12

It has been said,
"Happiness blooms from within."
I have found this to be true! How will you allow yourself
to experience happiness blooming
from within, today?

20__ _____

20__ _____

20__ _____

20__ _____

20__ _____

November 13

"A quiet secluded life in the country, with the possibility of being useful to people to whom it is easy to do good, and who are not accustomed to have it done to them; then work which one hopes may be of some use; then rest, nature, books, music, love for one's neighbor—such is my idea of happiness."
—Leo Tolstoy, ***Family Happiness***[46]

20__ _____

20__ _____

20__ _____

20__ _____

20__ _____

---

46. https://www.goodreads.com/quotes/64245-a-quiet-secluded-life-in-the-country-with-the-possibility Accessed 11 December 2021.

November 14

"Do not ask your children to strive for extraordinary lives. Such striving may seem admirable, but it is the way of foolishness. Help them instead to find the wonder and the marvel of an ordinary life. Show them the joy of tasting tomatoes, apples, and pears. Show them how to cry when pets and people die. Show them the infinite pleasure in the touch of a hand. And make the ordinary come alive for them. The extraordinary will take care of itself."
—William Martin,
***The Parent's Tao Te Ching:
Ancient Advice for Modern Parents***[47]

20__ _____

20__ _____

20__ _____

20__ _____

20__ _____

---

47. https://www.goodreads.com/quotes/505843-do-not-ask-your-children-to-strive-for-extraordinary-lives Accessed 27 July 2022.

November 15
How would you describe your
ideal external environment and home life?

20__ _____

20__ _____

20__ _____

20__ _____

20__ _____

Mrs. Valerie Christina Malicki, MA, LPCC, CPM

November 16
"Happiness is in the home."
—Anonymous

20__ _____

20__ _____

20__ _____

20__ _____

20__ _____

November 17

"It was so wonderful to be there,
safe at home, sheltered from the winds and the cold.
Laura thought that this must be a little like heaven,
where the weary are at rest."
—Laura Ingalls Wilder,
The Long Winter[48]

20__ _____

20__ _____

20__ _____

20__ _____

20__ _____

---

48. Laura Ingalls Wilder, ***The Long Winter***, Revised Edition illustrated by Garth Williams, (New York, New York: HarperCollins Publishers, Inc, 1953).

Mrs. Valerie Christina Malicki, MA, LPCC, CPM

November 18
How would it be for your home
to be a haven, a place to experience real rest?
As you ponder your nesting vision, I invite you to
expand your vision. What is one more way your external
environment may be more restful? How
would this change positively impact you and
your loved ones' experiences of
rest at home?

20__ _____

20__ _____

20__ _____

20__ _____

20__ _____

November 19

"The place where God calls you is the place where your deep gladness and the world's deep hunger meet."
—Frederick Buechner

20__ _____

20__ _____

20__ _____

20__ _____

20__ _____

November 20

"People often say that motivation doesn't last. Well, neither does bathing—that's why we recommend it daily."
—Zig Ziglar

(Many mothers would say the same about a clean laundry room, and home… it just doesn't last. Cleaning daily is needed for a home that is functional, especially in bigger families. We have found a little bit of daily chores with meals and laundry does go a long way, especially when everyone helps out.)

20__ _____

20__ _____

20__ _____

20__ _____

20__ _____

November 21

As seen on a jokester kitchen towel:
"Why do you people need to eat every day?!"

20__ _____

20__ _____

20__ _____

20__ _____

20__ _____

Mrs. Valerie Christina Malicki, MA, LPCC, CPM

November 22
"The way to avoid housework is to live outside."
—Sandra Blacksmith

20__ _____

20__ _____

20__ _____

20__ _____

20__ _____

November 23

"The homemaker has the ultimate career. All other careers exist for one purpose only—and that is to support the ultimate career."
—C.S. Lewis

20__ _____

20__ _____

20__ _____

20__ _____

20__ _____

Mrs. Valerie Christina Malicki, MA, LPCC, CPM

November 24
"God gives every bird its food,
but He does not throw it into its nest."
—Josiah Gilbert Holland

20__ _____

20__ _____

20__ _____

20__ _____

20__ _____

November 25

"There will come a time when you believe everything is finished; that will be the beginning."
—Louis L'Amour

20__ _____

20__ _____

20__ _____

20__ _____

20__ _____

Mrs. Valerie Christina Malicki, MA, LPCC, CPM

November 26

Having babies for a decade was such a wild season! As I said goodbye to this season, I realized clearly: it was only the beginning.

My husband and I had our tribe—The Malicki Six. Now, the tribe needed lots of daily TLC (Tender Loving Care), especially in our home. This rigorous work of dishes, laundry, bedtimes, and the like is all worth it as we enjoy fun daily adventures together. Each day is such an adventure, but it's a good adventure. I am so thankful for the loving, fun home we enjoy and create, and re-enjoy and re-create each day.

20__ _____

20__ _____

20__ _____

20__ _____

20__ _____

November 27

"There is only one adventurer in the world, as can be seen very clearly in the modern world: the father of a family. Even the most desperate adventurers are nothing compared with him. Everything in the modern world is organized against that fool, that imprudent, daring fool, against the unruly, audacious man who is daring enough to have a wife and family."
—Charles Péguy[49]

20__ _____

20__ _____

20__ _____

20__ _____

20__ _____

---

49. https://themanwhowouldbeknight.wordpress.com/2018/06/17/charles-peguy-on-fatherhood/ Accessed 11 December 2021.

Mrs. Valerie Christina Malicki, MA, LPCC, CPM

November 28

I would say both mother *and* father
are desperately brave adventurers. Thankfully, our
kids teach us many life lessons, daily! I especially love
witnessing and experiencing their free-spirited Joy. They
always seem to know how to have a good time. This
autumn, my son randomly asked to stop and get a huge
pumpkin. What a good idea, and what a fun way to savor
the pleasures of the season! It made me smile to see this
big, festive pumpkin sitting on our porch step. My son
always seems to know how to brighten my day in
simple, everyday ways that make me smile
and even giggle. A good thing!

For me, my daily nesting adventures
create the family memories I always dreamed of
experiencing. It's a steep climb at times, for sure. Yet, this
nesting experience of making lovely environments
within our own hearts, and "without"
(in our home), is all worth it.

20__ _____

20__ _____

20__ _____

20__ _____

20__ _____

November 29

"She is clothed with strength and dignity; she can laugh at the days to come."
—Proverbs 31:25, NIV

20__ _____

20__ _____

20__ _____

20__ _____

20__ _____

Mrs. Valerie Christina Malicki, MA, LPCC, CPM

November 30

We are coming to the end of our focus on nesting. Nesting means making our environments lovely, both within and on the outside. What is one way you have expanded your vision of nesting? How will you *enjoy* "being home," within your own heart, or in your external environment, today?

20__ _____

20__ _____

20__ _____

20__ _____

20__ _____

At Eve's Joy Professional Mentoring
we specialize in pastoral care for women only.

We offer a unique, world-class blend of
faith-based, therapeutically-informed, certified
professional mentoring.

We would love to hear more about your unique *nesting vision*, and also provide you with specific next steps on how to continue to make it happen.

Simply drop us your current one-sentence *nesting vision* at EvesJoy.com. You can leave your confidential vision at the bottom of the home page where it says "Leave a message." With this simple entry, you apply to receive one of our periodic, free, confidential, exploration calls. An exploration call is guaranteed to be the best next step toward creating your own
unique *nesting vision*.

Your completely confidential response helps
us to create content that further supports you, such as:
blogs, emails, webinars, summit/retreat topics, new online groups, podcasts, et cetera.

We are constantly creating new supportive content for you. Please drop us a line and let us know how we can support your next step toward becoming a woman of Wild Joy!

DECEMBER

Become a Woman of Wild Joy
Through *Celebrating*.

"The consolation of fairy-stories, the joy of the happy ending; or more correctly of the good catastrophe, the sudden joyous 'turn' (for there is no true end to any fairy-tale): this joy, which is one of the things which fairy-stories can produce supremely well, is not essentially 'escapist,' nor 'fugitive.' In its fairy-tale—or otherworld—setting, it is a sudden and miraculous grace: never to be counted on to recur. It does not deny the existence of dyscatastrophe, of sorrow and failure: the possibility of these is necessary to the joy of deliverance; it denies (in the face of much evidence, if you will) universal final defeat and in so far is evangelium, giving a fleeting glimpse of Joy, Joy beyond the walls of the world, poignant as grief."
—J.R.R. Tolkien, *Tolkien On Fairy-stories*[50]

If your life were a fairy-story, what would you most need to happen, right now, for you to experience your "happily ever after"? Would you need: success in your work endeavors, romantic love, more fun, playful free time, greater creativity time, spiritual growth, greater influence, impact, prosperity, and/or close, safe, emotionally connected relationships?

---

50. https://www.goodreads.com/work/quotes/58418323-tolkien-on-fairy-stories Accessed 19 February 2022.

How would a good catastrophe *best* occur, for you, these days? What is your own happily ever after, your own "good catastrophe"?

Imagine the next month of your life being titled: "Celebration." What do you see, smell, taste, hear, and feel? Take 15 minutes to be still, and with focused intention, visualize your answers. Imagine living your own happily ever after, your own fairy tale, every day.

Simply finish the following sentence below, today, and then each consecutive year:

My own happily ever after looks like:

20__ _____

20__ _____

20__ _____

20__ _____

20__ _____

This is your unique *celebration vision*.
As we journey together each day in December, let's stay focused by remembering our mantra:
I become a woman of Wild Joy through *celebrating*.

Mrs. Valerie Christina Malicki, MA, LPCC, CPM

December 1

Imagine the heroine of your own unique fairy tale. I imagine that the heroine of my fairy tale is wonderfully resilient, magnetic, and brilliant! What superpowers, or character strengths, would enable your own heroine to hold the paradox of "happily ever after" and "real life," too? I invite you to imagine *being* this heroine, today and all month!

20__ _____

20__ _____

20__ _____

20__ _____

20__ _____

December 2

"God rewrote the text of my life."
—Psalm 18, TMT

How would you love for the
text of your own life to be rewritten?

20__ _____

20__ _____

20__ _____

20__ _____

20__ _____

December 3

"But even now I know this isn't a fairy tale. I know that we'll have hard times, confusing times. I know that things won't always happen the way we want them to and that we'll have to work to remember that we chose this. It won't be perfect, not all the time.

This isn't happily ever after.

It's so much more than that."

—Kiera Cass, *The One (The Selection, #3)*[51]

20__ _____

20__ _____

20__ _____

20__ _____

20__ _____

---

51. https://www.goodreads.com/work/quotes/21587145-the-one Accessed 24 May 2022.

December 4

Twenty years ago, God called me to be a flourishing woman, wife, and mom. Was this even possible, or just a college fantasy? Many times along the journey, it all certainly seemed rather impossible.

In what ways do you yearn to flourish?

20__ _____

20__ _____

20__ _____

20__ _____

20__ _____

Mrs. Valerie Christina Malicki, MA, LPCC, CPM

December 5

"So many of our dreams at first seem impossible, then they seem improbable, and then, when we summon the will, they soon become inevitable."
—Christopher Reeve

How would you describe
the stage that your dream is in these days?

20__ _____

20__ _____

20__ _____

20__ _____

20__ _____

December 6

These days, I am amazed that my husband and I really have created our li'l tribe, The Malicki Six. This has been, and continues to be, the adventure of a lifetime. At times, it has been a treacherously steep climb. Even so, I am deeply thankful to be surrounded by our loving family, especially at celebration times.

I *celebrate* that I know, from experience, this truth: "the steeper the climb, the better the view!" We *celebrate* many precious moments these days, and my heart bursts with Joy—Wild Joy!
God is so good!

20__ _____

20__ _____

20__ _____

20__ _____

20__ _____

Mrs. Valerie Christina Malicki, MA, LPCC, CPM

December 7

"Twenty years from now you will be more disappointed by the things that you didn't do than by the ones you did do. So throw off the bowlines. Sail away from the safe harbor. Catch the trade winds in your sails. Explore. Dream. Discover."
—Mark Twain

How does the heroine of your own fairy tale story yearn to explore, dream, and discover, today?

20__ _____

20__ _____

20__ _____

20__ _____

20__ _____

December 8

"Eventually all things fall into place. Until then, laugh at the confusion, live for the moments, and know *everything happens for a reason*."
—Albert Schweitzer

What is one moment in your life that was troubling and confusing…and yet, you now better understand some reasons that it may have happened? How did everything fall right into place?

20__ _____

20__ _____

20__ _____

20__ _____

20__ _____

December 9

"Puff puff, chug chug.
Up the mountain went Little Blue Engine.
And all the time she kept saying, 'I think I can, I think I can, I think I can...' Up, up, up. The little engine climbed and climbed."
-Watty Piper,
Adapted for young readers by Walter Retan,
The Little Engine That Could[52]

20__ _____

20__ _____

20__ _____

20__ _____

20__ _____

---

52. Piper, Watty, Adapted for young readers by Walter Retan, ***The Little Engine That Could***, (New York, New York: Penguin Group USA LLC, 1986).

December 10

"in the end, she became more than what she expected. she became the journey, and like all journeys, she did not end, she just simply changed directions and kept going."
—r.m.drake[53]

20__ _____

20__ _____

20__ _____

20__ _____

20__ _____

---

53. https://www.yourtango.com/2016296367/15-heart-stopping-instagram-quotes-poet-r-m-drake-about-life Accessed 19 August 2022.

Mrs. Valerie Christina Malicki, MA, LPCC, CPM

December 11

"We've been overwhelmed with grief; come now and overwhelm us with gladness. Replace our years of trouble with decades of delight. Let us see your miracles again, and let the rising generation see the glorious wonders you're famous for. O Lord our God, let your sweet beauty rest upon us and give us favor. Come work with us, and then our works will endure, and give us success in all we do."
—Psalm 90:15-17, TPT

20__ _____

20__ _____

20__ _____

20__ _____

20__ _____

December 12

"It is like when you throw a stone into a pool, and the concentric waves spread out further and further. Who knows where it will end? Redeemed humanity is still young, it has hardly come to its full strength. But already there is joy enough in the little finger of a great saint such as yonder lady to waken all the dead things of the universe into life."
—C.S. Lewis, ***The Great Divorce***[54]

20__ _____

20__ _____

20__ _____

20__ _____

20__ _____

---

54. C.S. Lewis, ***The Great Divorce*** (New York: Macmillan Publishing Company, 1946).

Mrs. Valerie Christina Malicki, MA, LPCC, CPM

December 13

"It has been a wonderful experience to compete in the Olympic Games and to bring home a gold medal. But since I have been a young lad, I have had my eyes on a different prize. You see, each one of us is in a greater race than any I have run in Paris, and this race ends when God gives out
the medals."
—Eric Liddell[55]

20__ _____

20__ _____

20__ _____

20__ _____

20__ _____

---

55. https://www.goodreads.com/author/quotes/802465.Eric_Liddell Accessed 13 February 2022.

December 14

Your life in five years will be determined by your actions this year, this month, this day, this hour. My friend, I invite you to experience Wild Joy today by *celebrating* your successes, and by chasing your wildest dreams! What, and how, would you love to *celebrate* in your life in five years? What is your next step today?

20__ _____

20__ _____

20__ _____

20__ _____

20__ _____

Mrs. Valerie Christina Malicki, MA, LPCC, CPM

December 15
"The best way to predict the future is to create it."
—Abraham Lincoln

What is your next action step, today, toward creating the future of your wildest dreams?

20__ _____

20__ _____

20__ _____

20__ _____

20__ _____

December 16
"Is anything too hard for the Lord?"
—Genesis 18:14a, NIV

20__ _____

20__ _____

20__ _____

20__ _____

20__ _____

Mrs. Valerie Christina Malicki, MA, LPCC, CPM

December 17

"It's kind of fun to do the impossible."
—Walt Disney

What are a few further details of your own "good catastrophe" story? In order to fully experience this amazing dream, what other superpowers would the heroine (that's you!) implement?

I love that the heroine of my "good catastrophe" fairy-story is a creative financial genius!

20__ _____

20__ _____

20__ _____

20__ _____

20__ _____

December 18

"Christmas waves a magic wand
over the world, and behold, everything is
softer and more beautiful."
—Norman Vincent Peale

In what way would a magic wand make
everything in your world softer and more beautiful?

20__ _____

20__ _____

20__ _____

20__ _____

20__ _____

December 19
"Gifts of time and love are surely the basic ingredients of a truly merry Christmas."
—Peg Bracken

20__ _____

20__ _____

20__ _____

20__ _____

20__ _____

December 20

"Then the Grinch thought of something he hadn't before! What if Christmas, he thought, doesn't come from a store. What if Christmas... perhaps...means a little bit more!"
—Dr. Seuss, ***How the Grinch Stole Christmas!***[56]

20__ _____

20__ _____

20__ _____

20__ _____

20__ _____

---

56. Dr. Seuss, ***How the Grinch Stole Christmas!***, copyright 1957, renewed 1985 by Dr. Seuss Enterprises, L.P., a title contained in ***Your Favorite Seuss***, compiled by Janet Schulman and Cathy Goldsmith (New York: Random House, 2004).

Mrs. Valerie Christina Malicki, MA, LPCC, CPM

December 21

"There are always miracles in the world, even when all seems hopeless. And when there are no miracles, you can make them happen."
—Eddie Jaku, ***The Happiest Man On Earth: The Beautiful Life of an Auschwitz Survivor***[57]

What miracle would you love to help make happen this December?

20__ _____

20__ _____

20__ _____

20__ _____

20__ _____

---

57. Eddie Jaku, ***The Happiest Man On Earth: The Beautiful Life of an Auschwitz Survivor***, (New York, NY: Harper an Imprint of HarperCollins Publishers, 2021).

December 22

"The holiest of all holidays are those kept by ourselves in silence and apart, the secret anniversaries of the heart, when the full tide of feeling overflows."
—Henry Wadsworth Longfellow[58]

Another way to celebrate the holiday season for me is to reflect back on the past year. I remember my own anniversaries of the heart, and all that the past year has meant to me. I remember hard lessons learned, and good lessons learned.

What memory from the past year brings a full tide of feelings for you?

20__ _____

20__ _____

20__ _____

20__ _____

20__ _____

---

58. https://quotefancy.com/quote/826709/Henry-Wadsworth-Longfellow-The-holiest-of-holidays-are-those-kept-by-ourselves-in-silence Accessed 14 February 2022.

December 23

"Were I a philosopher, I should write a philosophy of toys, showing that nothing else in life need to be taken seriously, and that Christmas Day in the company of children is one of the few occasions on which men become entirely alive."
—Robert Lynd[59]

20__ _____

20__ _____

20__ _____

20__ _____

20__ _____

---

59. https://www.goodreads.com/author/show/46890.Robert_Lynd Accessed 13 February 2022.

December 24

"Uncles and aunts, and cousins,
are all very well, and fathers and mothers
are not to be despised; but a grandmother, at
holiday time, is worth them all."
—Fanny Fern[60]

20__ _____

20__ _____

20__ _____

20__ _____

20__ _____

---

60. https://www.legacyproject.org/guides/gptoday.html Accessed 19 August 2022.

Mrs. Valerie Christina Malicki, MA, LPCC, CPM

December 25

Our four children certainly remind us, daily, of the philosophy of fun and play. For me, being surrounded by these young little loved ones is a rewarding way to celebrate Christmas.

As the year ends, I especially imagine how I want to experience celebration in the next year. (At times, I imagine that one day I'll be celebrating Christmas with *all* our children *and* grandchildren!)

How would you want to experience celebration today, and in the future?

20__ _____

20__ _____

20__ _____

20__ _____

20__ _____

December 26

"Last year's words belong to last
year's language. And next year's words
await another voice."
—T.S. Eliot

What are a few words you are ready to bid farewell as this year comes to a close? Perhaps you are saying goodbye to draining words that describe experiences of sadness, lack, or isolation. Perhaps instead you are saying hello to positive, life-affirming words and experiences, such as joy, abundance, or connection. Be curious. Explore a few words you would love to focus on —and experience—in the upcoming year.

20__ _____

20__ _____

20__ _____

20__ _____

20__ _____

December 27

"Laura felt a warmth inside her. It was very small, but it was strong. It was steady, like a tiny light in the dark, and it burned very low but no winds could make it flicker because it would not give up."
—Laura Ingalls Wilder, ***The Long Winter***[61]

20__ _____

20__ _____

20__ _____

20__ _____

20__ _____

---

61. Laura Ingalls Wilder, ***The Long Winter***, Revised Edition illustrated by Garth Williams, (New York, New York: HarperCollins Publishers, Inc, 1953).

December 28

I invite you to *celebrate* that God can rewrite the text of your life, as you call out to Him in prayer, as you open yourself to experiencing His Divine Redemption, and as you grow and transform your life, love, and legacy.

I invite you to allow yourself to imagine feeling the sudden and miraculously good turn of events, this happy ending to your own story. Take a moment to let it all sink in!

And then, let's ponder, together.
What is the best, most unique, and personal lesson you have learned this month as you imagined yourself being the heroine of your own "good catastrophe" fairy tale?

20__ _____

20__ _____

20__ _____

20__ _____

20__ _____

December 29

Voila! You! You are! You are here! You are here, now! You are here now, experiencing trials, travails, *and* triumphs! If the very best, most supportive kind of mentor in the whole world would *celebrate* the ways you are growing, changing, and transforming, what would they say to you today? (In what way do you need to be encouraged, cheered on, and championed in your journey?)

20__ _____

20__ _____

20__ _____

20__ _____

20__ _____

December 30

"When you realize how perfect everything is, you will tilt your head back and laugh at the sky."
—Anonymous

20__ _____

20__ _____

20__ _____

20__ _____

20__ _____

Mrs. Valerie Christina Malicki, MA, LPCC, CPM

December 31

Remember: You are doing a great job!
Good things are coming! Never, ever, ever, give up!

As we end this month's focus, I invite you
to realize and *celebrate* all the empowerment,
transformation, and Wild Joy that is truly a part of your
life these days. I invite you to *celebrate* all
that is, and all that will be.

Ponder something that makes you throw
your head back and laugh at the sky! Whoohoo!

I invite you to experience Wild Joy through *celebrating*
today and to *never* forget... *You got this!*

20__ _____

20__ _____

20__ _____

20__ _____

20__ _____

At Eve's Joy Professional Mentoring
we specialize in pastoral care for women only.

We offer a unique, world-class blend of faith-based, therapeutically-informed, certified professional mentoring.

We would love to hear more about your unique *celebration vision*, and also provide you with specific next steps on how to continue to make it happen.

Simply drop us your current one-sentence *celebration vision* at EvesJoy.com. You can leave your confidential vision at the bottom of the home page where it says "Leave a message." With this simple entry, you apply to receive one of our periodic, free, confidential, exploration calls. An exploration call is guaranteed to be the best next step toward creating your own
unique *celebration vision*.

Your completely confidential response helps us to create content that further supports you, such as: blogs, emails, webinars, summit/retreat topics, new online groups, podcasts, et cetera.

We are constantly creating new supportive content for you. Please drop us a line and let us know how we can support your next step toward becoming a woman of Wild Joy!

Acknowledgements

Thank you to the team at Self Publishing School, especially Kerk M., for believing in me. That in itself is a huge gift. Thank you for not laughing at my wild ideas. I would not be here, as a published author, without this remarkable team! Thank you for standing for my wild success.

Thank you to all the people who worked behind the scenes with formatting, editing, cover design, and many unimaginable and necessary details, details, and more details. Wow, all the pieces of the puzzle have come together. Thank you for your professionalism!

Thank you to all my friends at the Christian and Missionary Alliance church. A special thank you to Donna K. for playing matchmaker with Russ and I, over 17 years ago. It only takes a spark to get a fire going. Thank you to Grace W. for brilliant matriarch inspo and positive, kind support! Thank you to Jim and Crystal S. for nearly five decades of marital bliss inspo and for bringing ice cream to the summer parties. Thank you to Barb P. for beautifully encouraging and loving cards, written in violet ink, of course. Thank you to Sharon P. for thoughtfulness to our whole tribe on anniversaries and birthdays—with actual, mailed cards. Wow! Thank you to Joni for weekly pretzels, goodies, and for many simple, thoughtful kindnesses. Also a special thank you to Candace M. for being a homeschooling exemplar who responds to my random inquiries. I appreciate this! Thank you all for showing God's Love in word and especially in deed.

Thank you to Hiram S.
for supporting my big dreams and for affirming my calling as a writer and mentor. We all need sunshine to grow.
Thanks H.

Thank you Linda M.
for supporting our family, and especially supporting us to be strong and brave. Every card and kindness is appreciated.
Thank you!

Thank you to Paul C.
for all the chitter chatter. Haha, our convos are awesome and I appreciate each one.
God bless you!

Thank you to Elaine B.
for supporting me and especially for living so many stories with me, in your life, and even in your death. Your life makes a mark, E.

Thank you to Dan M.
for accepting the challenge of passing on good, memorable camping times with the grandchildren. I envision the wild, wooly, pirate stories living on to the next generation. Ha!

Thank you to Dale S.
for a magnificent farm in which to write, live, love, and laugh. It is unbelievable that you and Mom purchased our home when I was a child, and that it rather strangely worked out for my own family to enjoy the legacy that is here, every day. We all love and appreciate our hidden, homeschooling, homesteading life.
Thank you, Dad.

Thank you to my hubby Russ.
Thank you for saying, and showing, that you'd do anything for me. Thank you for being a loyal and loving life mate. The best is yet to come, baba. (We made it through four babies and a surprise at-home birth together. We can do *anything*, now! Haha!)

Thank you to
Rosie, Violet, Milo, and Lilac M.
for being my biggest fans, and for giving me so many good, spectacular, everyday—and true—stories. I couldn't ask for better children. Wow! Thank you, as Rosie says, for being my "teachers." You are the best teachers!!

Thank you to countless friends, family, connections, and literal strangers along the journey who have become part of my soul tribe. You are all deeply appreciated. Especially you who say that naming you here… is unnecessary. I appreciate all support and know that every friend is a treasure… to be treasured. Thank you for the enduring and positive support! Yes, we all need sunshine to grow. Thanks for lifting me up. Together we really are stronger! Thank you to my soul tribe. You know who you are! Blessings!!

Excited to see the next chapters
of all our stories. Let's all keep living, laughing, and loving each day. God bless you all in a mighty way!!

With Love and Gratitude, Valerie

A Closing Encouragement
To Be Blessed and Be a Blessing

I hope and pray that, in reading this book,
you have been blessed, and that you will pass on the
blessing in your life, love, and legacy.

If this book has blessed
you, I would be so *appreciative* if you share an
authentic online review where you purchased
this book.

Your review may be the reason that
more people hear about this book, and that more lives,
loves, and legacies can be transformed forever.

Thank you in advance for being a blessing!
God bless you!!

About the author's professional credentials:
Mrs. Valerie Christina Malicki, MA, LPCC, CPM, has been a licensed therapist since her 20s, having graduated from Ashland Theological Seminary, a division of Ashland University, with a Master's degree in pastoral clinical counseling. The MA stands for Master of Arts in Pastoral Clinical Counseling. The LPCC stands for Licensed Professional Clinical Counselor. Her training in human development, spirituality, and soul care began at age 17 at Wheaton College, where she earned a bachelor of arts degree in Christian Education. CPM stands for Certified Professional Mentor. She has culminated over two decades of professional training, personal lived experiences of marriage and motherhood, and therapeutic skills into the art of professional mentoring. She is the CEO of Eve's Joy Professional Mentoring. Eve's Joy offers a unique, world-class blend of faith-based, therapeutically-informed, certified professional mentoring. Eve's Joy specializes in pastoral care for women only.

Valerie is actually best described as a Daughter of The King, a Visionary American Woman, a Lover of 17 years to her Husband and Fellow Family Adventurer, a Homeschooler of four Blessings, an Off-Grid Free-Spirited Girl, a Homesteader, and the CEO at Eve's Joy Professional Mentoring, EvesJoy.com. She is an eighth-generation Midwest country girl, a corn farmer's daughter, and an unplugged, free-spirited girl who grew up as Valerie Smith. What she would (sometimes) rather be doing is unplugging and going on a loooong country walk, with her long, dirty blonde hair in a baseball cap or messy bun, and then chilling under her tree (named Mr. Cedar) whilst writing in one of her maaaany journals. She loves to live the hidden, homeschooling, homesteading life with her tribe, The Malicki Six, in her farmhouse home.

Valerie's personal side can, at times, be seen on:

Fb: MrsValerie Malicki
Gab: MrsValerie Malicki
Pinterest: MrsValerie Malicki
Youtube: MrsValerie Malicki
Instagram: MrsValerie Malicki
Twitter: MrsValerie Malicki
Telegram: MrsValerie Malicki
LinkedIn: MrsValerie Malicki
Rumble: MrsValerie Malicki
Substack: MrsValerie Malicki

At Eve's Joy Professional Mentoring
we offer unique, specialized support in helping women discover the surprising delights of marriage, motherhood, and their life mission.

We offer a unique, world-class blend of faith-based, therapeutically-informed, certified professional mentoring that elevates a woman's life, love, and legacy forever.

Subscribing at EvesJoy.com for exclusive updates, offers, &events is your *next step* on your journey of becoming a woman of Wild Joy.

Simply scroll to the bottom of the Home page at EvesJoy.com, where it says SUBSCRIBE.

Eve's Joy provides a personalized, FREE email newsletter to all subscribers. We offer a variety of services, at a variety of support levels. I would love to get to know you better and discover ways to better support you in your own journey.

Our mission at Eve's Joy Professional Mentoring is to empower 1,000,000 women who will then empower 1,000,000 families, then communities, and then nations, and then, the world.

By subscribing for FREE at Eve's Joy Professional Mentoring, you join us on our mission to empower YOU! Looking forward to staying in touch.
God bless you!

It has been said,
"The steeper the climb, the better the view."

A woman with a vision for her life, love, and legacy is a woman who needs strength. She can be strengthened on her own unique, steep climb with the transformative power of Wild Joy.

If you are picking up this book, you are well on your way to becoming a woman of Wild Joy. This journal is your personal, 21st century guide to a loving marriage, beautiful motherhood, and *your* life mission. Let this book encourage your heart daily to remember the vision you have for *your* life, love, and legacy.

Together, we will reflect upon desires and clarify our life mission. We will explore mentorship, connection, attachment, Joy in work, repairing the past, and daringly facing the future. Together we will rise, and soar, and then settle in and happily "nest," by being "home." Together we will throw our pretty heads back and laugh at the sky. We will rejoice with deep gratitude in how very blessed we are. Together, we will discover surprising delights every step of the way of marriage, motherhood, and life mission.

Yes, welcome, welcome, welcome!
Can't wait to see ya in the "Intro," beautiful friend!

Made in the USA
Monee, IL
26 June 2023

37429926R00252